FIRST
CATCH YOUR PIG!

REAL COOKING WITH REAL INGREDIENTS FROM THE KITCHEN OF

THE MILESTONE

Written by:

Matt Bigland, Marc Sheldon,
Simon Ayres, James Wallis at:

The Milestone
84 Green Lane at Ball Street
Kelham Island, Sheffield S3 8SE
Telephone (0114) 272 8327

Edited by:

Martin Edwards,
Karen Horsefield, Chris Brierley
RMC Books – (0114) 250 6300

Design by:

Paul Cocker
RMC Books – (0114) 250 6300

Photography by:

Jodi Hinds – www.jodihinds.com

Contributors:

Ben Fowler, Victoria Philpott,
Max Feetham, Elaine Wallis

THE MILESTONE

First Published in 2010 on behalf of:
The Milestone
www.the-milestone.co.uk

RMC BOOKS

Published by:
RMC Books – www.rmcbooks.co.uk

CONTENTS

STARTERS

MAIN COURSES

DESSERTS

BASIC RECIPES

Acknowledgments

Firstly, we would like to thank our parents for their unconditional love and support!

Matt would particularly like to thank my beautiful wife Nina for believing in The Milestone from the very beginning and putting up with the daily dramas thrown up by the business that often pulls me away from family life. For that you're amazing!

The team, without them none of this would be possible. For coming in every day with passion and belief in the brand and for creating chaos on every staff night out - we love you all!

Special thanks goes to our senior chefs Simon Ayres and James Wallis, who helped shape this book and the journey we have all been on together which has made us who we are today. As Gordon Ramsay said; "Four Yorkshire young guns!" The intensity of Ramsay's Best Restaurant made us closer. We thank you for being fantastic friends, as well as colleagues.

We would also like to say a big thank you to our maintenance manager who comes in every Saturday and gives everything but asks for nothing except a cup of tea, a bacon butty and some lively banter..."What's happening??!!"

Finally, we'd especially like to thank our loyal guests who have seen The Milestone evolve over the last 4 years. We thank you all for your support and valuable feedback, without you we would not be where we are today!

We look forward to what the future holds- it's shit or bust!

Lots of love

Matt 'Biggi' Bigland & Marc 'Bulldog' Sheldon x

Introduction

We think Mrs Beeton would have approved.

In borrowing and adapting one of her most famous phrases as the title of this book, we touched on something both we and the great-grandma of cooking believe in.

Back in Mrs B's day, cooking meant being close to the raw ingredients. There was no supermarket, no supply chain, and no wholesaler. You either grew or reared them, or you went to the local market and squeezed, tasted and haggled over them. It's something we have lost, and it's an issue that matters to us at The Milestone.

So, as well as tried-and-tested recipes from our kitchens, the following pages say a lot about a principle we take seriously.

Mixing heritage with modernity is the driving force at The Milestone. Housed in the oldest industrial site in Sheffield, we serve dishes that stir up memories and awaken the taste buds. In our Victorian pub we resurrect the best of the old and marry it with the new, just like the listed building which we chose to realise our vision, once forgotten and derelict, now brought lovingly back to life.

The hero of The Milestone story is, of course, our food and we take meticulous care to source it locally – or create it ourselves. We use the freshest vegetables – from local allotment growers when we can, pork from our own rare breed herd of pigs, meat from local farms, game from the vast moors nearby and fish from the British coast. We don't buy anything if we can make it ourselves, including bread, pasta, chutneys and ice cream.

The faster fresh food gets cooked, the better it tastes. It's not unknown for us to change the entire menu if we have an unexpected delivery of outstanding meat or vegetables. Once we spent a whole night preparing mackerel that had been line-caught by the grandad of one of our staff. Another day we downed tools to pluck two pheasants brought in by a local farmer. It's a privilege to be able to use such quality food; we deliver its unique flavour fresh on the plate, just as it's supposed to taste.

There's been a lot of swagger in the restaurant industry about using seasonal, local produce, but at The Milestone we genuinely put our money where our mouth is. Every ingredient in our dishes can be traced to its source. We don't think buying food from our close surroundings is extraordinary or trendy: it just makes good sense. Our ancestors created dishes in tune with the seasons for centuries, but we've lost touch with this basic practice and sacrifice flavour for convenience. If a grower arrives at The Milestone with a car boot full of rhubarb or runner beans, we create something around those ingredients and put it straight on the menu. Nature provides when it's ready and we respect that. Our philosophy on freshness extends to the meats we use, including game in season shot by a local farmer.

We also bow to tradition in many of our cooking methods. We pride ourselves on reintroducing unloved cuts to our diners including sweetbreads, brisket, beef cheek and pig's trotters. These meats need plenty of attention and slow cooking to yield unbelievable depths of flavour and succulence.

In fact, our experience of taking our first delivery of two un-butchered pigs from our herd taught us a great lesson: to use every part of the animal from trotters to tail. That week's menu centred on pork recipes created by our chefs, some of which, like pig's head, were so popular they became regular dishes. We applied the same rules to other meats and started to run 'Nose to Tail' and fish weeks in the gastropub throughout the year. Out of these thematic menus a range of fantastic recipes was born, some of which we include in this book.

Some restaurants bring out the worst in their owners: they're stuffy and snobby, worshipping at the altar of fine dining. We're operating in Yorkshire where people aren't impressed with window-dressing if the substance isn't there. We believe people should be able to eat food of superlative quality (and plenty of it) in a relaxed atmosphere.

The pared-down chic of our upstairs restaurant provides the perfect backdrop for its menu, featuring more intricate and technique-based dishes with a large helping of playfulness. Here we can show off the talents of our chefs with beautifully cooked and presented food. In the gastropub with its cosy décor, we serve more familiar, robust dishes, but always with our trademark twist.

Cooking in your own home splits itself into roughly the same categories: we all have to prepare everyday meals, but there are times when we want to step up the effort. Whatever the level of preparation and cooking involved, we think there's something here for everyone in this book, from the no-frills basic cook to the die-hard foodie. Alongside recipes for our most popular dishes is information about sourcing, seasonality and cooking techniques.

Above all, we believe cooking should be about fun and experimentation. Our kitchen is constantly trying new things and evolving original ways to serve up the finest ingredients. The end result is subjective. That's why none of our recipes are set in stone. Just try out a recipe, give it a taste and add a bit more flavour here and there. There are no rules. Our inspiration is simple: to bring out the best from the ingredients. We hope this book enthuses you to do the same.

Marc Sheldon & Matt Bigland

The Milestone at Kelham Island

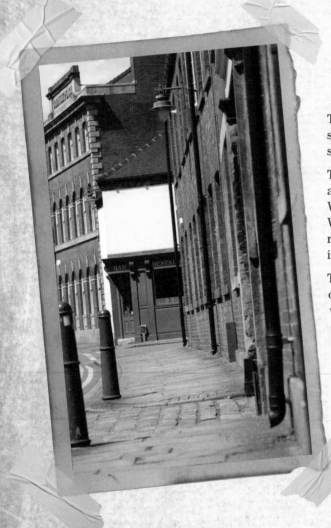

The Milestone site has housed a pub for over 170 years. It started life as The Ball Inn, set up in 1833 to cater for steelworkers at Kelham Island.

The building survived the disastrous Sheffield Flood of 1864 and went on serving local ales and food for another century. With the demise of the steel industry, the pub fell into disuse. We had the chance to buy the beautiful corner building and rescue it from obscurity and this opportunity was the impetus for starting our business.

The man-made island adjacent to The Milestone was created over 900 years ago by a mill course. Over the centuries, small workshops grew into enormous factories and huge buildings of brick, glass and steel replaced rolling green meadows. The area was the booming heart of Sheffield's early industrial revolution and The Ball Inn was one of many pubs filled with the chatter of this vibrant working community.

After years of neglect, Kelham Island is now being restored; modern housing and commercial developments sit alongside factories and light industry, including one of the oldest scissor-making firms in the country. And of course nearby Kelham Island Industrial Museum is filled with information about the history of this landmark location.

We are proud to be associated with the regeneration of an area that boasts such impressive heritage and architecture; for us, it's the perfect location to recreate a traditional venue for the modern market.

Teamwork

As a home cook, you have something in common with restaurant chefs like me: you're looking for inspiration. Whether you're seeking challenging recipes or want to build some basic culinary skills, there's something for you in this book. The Milestone provides the perfect environment to create imaginative dishes, thanks to the availability of fabulous seasonal ingredients and a kitchen that's constantly buzzing with new ideas. I'm fortunate to have James Wallis as a right-hand man, an excellent head chef who is alive to modern trends and new methods of presentation. His on-trend style is the perfect foil for my classically trained, old school approach. We work harmoniously, learning from one another but our techniques are different. If you're an observant diner, you'll even be able to guess which chef was responsible for the way your food looks on the plate in the restaurant.

This book, like our kitchen, is a fusion of the old and the new, containing the most popular recipes from our menus, with the emphasis on British food using ingredients in season that are easy or fun to find.

When was the last time you nosed around the great outdoors to find something for dinner? As chefs at The Milestone, we take our remit to produce fabulous fresh food seriously. Even if that involves scouting Endcliffe Park in the summer for elderflowers to team up with crayfish in a veloute or putting on gloves to grab ingredients for a nettle and wild mushroom cannelloni. Wild garlic, chickweed, girolles, sweet cicely, sorrel and flowers all find their way into our dishes throughout the warmer months when nature gives generously. But you needn't go far afield to find exciting produce; it can start on your own doorstep.

A burgeoning number of gardeners grow their own, from simple stuff like beans, peas, herbs and potatoes to greenhouse-dependent salad leaves, tomatoes and courgettes. We're always happy for new growers to get in touch and at the moment we're looking for a local mushroom forager.

Not everyone has the time, space or inclination to grow vegetables, but if you want to ensure the best flavour, buy fruit and veg in season at your greengrocer's or farmers' market, that way you're experiencing food as it's intended to taste. Nothing beats a fresh tomato soup or consomme, oozing with an evocative summer greenhouse aroma. Great tomatoes, berries, and orchard fruits may not be available all year round, but like British asparagus, garden peas, strawberries, salad leaves and crunchy radishes, they are worth waiting for. The same principle applies to the meats we use, whether from our own herd of pigs, newly-shot game or chicken, beef and lamb from local farmers, we give every cut the time it needs to be hung, cured or cooked in a way guaranteed to maximise taste.

Another golden rule in The Milestone kitchen is that nothing ever goes to waste, so in times of plenty, fruit and veg surplus is used to create stock or make chutneys, jams and pickles.

Our prudent attitude to food is best exemplified by the way we use more unusual parts of the animal and couch unfamiliar cuts in recognisable dishes. For example, we make a cottage pie made with sweetbreads rather than beef mince; cod cheek with chips and cannelloni with pheasant breast, rabbit leg and pig's tail. We've been enormously successful in reintroducing unloved cuts and offal because our recipes make them the champions of the plate, rather than the Cinderellas of the kitchen. A quick chat with your butcher and a bit of confidence is all you need to cook these meats in your own kitchen.

Even familiar staples like roast chicken can provide up to five meals if used wisely. Most people get their bird out of the oven, carve it badly then throw the carcass away, rather than using surplus leg and wing meat for rissoles, stirfries or curries and boiling the bones for a brilliant stock. We've scattered our recipes with canny tips to getting the most out of your food, in terms of flavour and value for money.

We enjoy producing and cooking new recipes, but we couldn't have developed our repertoire without the rest of the kitchen team. We can afford to be innovative because we have a dependable, enthusiastic crew around us who take the preparation of completely novel dishes in their stride.

This book is guided by our own cooking principles, while remaining conscious of your more limited time in the kitchen and access to ingredients. From simple everyday meals to more technique-based feasts, we hope our book will make cooking more enjoyable, responsible – and fun.

Senior Head Chef Simon Ayres and the team at The Milestone

Hand reared

A friend and I regularly met for Saturday breakfast at various cafés and restaurants around Sheffield and we always ended up bemoaning the poor quality of the meat on our plates. I decided I could probably do a better job myself and hit on the idea of rearing my own pigs to guarantee decent sausages, bacon and other cuts. It might sound a bit extreme, but pigkeeping turned into an absorbing hobby over time. I went into partnership with a friend, Andrew Hardman, who owns an arable farm at Grenoside, and Andrew's sister Wendy Duggan.

We did some research which led us to the Godfather of pigkeeping, Tony York. Tony is the oracle on pigs and lectures on them to the Royal Veterinary College. We went on one of his weekend courses in Wiltshire to find out how to set ourselves up properly, manage the pigs and keep them healthy.

After that it was a case of building the pens, registering with DEFRA and the local authority and finding some piglets. We started with 7 at first and over the past couple of years that number has fluctuated up to 15. We get the piglets when they've been weaned naturally at about 8 weeks (by comparison, commercial pigs are taken from their mothers at just 3 weeks). We feed them on barley porridge, and slightly overripe fruit and vegetables from the local post office. Their favourites are strawberries and bananas.

There are so many different breeds of pigs; we've kept Large Blacks, Oxford Sandy and Black and Berkshires, but our favourites are probably Gloucester Old Spots, a rare breed with enormous floppy ears. They have great personalities and are very tame; they never try to bite and roll over on their backs for you to scratch them.

Historically, Gloucester Old Spots roamed orchards, feeding on windfalls and folklore has it that their spots are bruises caused from falling apples. Above all, they produce excellent quality pork.

Our pigs are slaughtered at 26 weeks for pork and leaner cuts and at 35 weeks for bacon, ham and gammon. That's because in those 9 weeks, pigs lay down from 30-50lb and their meat changes subtly in flavour. We don't artificially fatten our pigs by giving them growth hormones and they're free to roam around and exercise. For that reason, they take twice as long to reach weight as commercially reared pigs, but our meat is leaner and much more tasty than anything you'd get in a supermarket.

We don't sell our meat to anyone apart from family and friends. Our connection with The Milestone began as I'm a regular customer and think it's one of the best restaurants in Sheffield. I had a good idea they'd be interested in our small operation because locally produced free-range pork ties in perfectly with their ethos. The owners Matt and Marc were impressed with our set up and could see our pigs were living the high life. What's more, the pork these pigs produce is second to none. Now we rear pigs for the restaurant according to their requirements.

We didn't intend to breed pigs here, but it's the next obvious step. We put our two gilts (virgin female pigs) with a hired boar recently and are hoping for litters from them in the near future. We've looked into different breeding and rearing methods and recently spent time at Chatsworth Farm to see their very successful programme.

In the meantime we continue to buy weaners from all over the country. We've travelled from County Durham to Lincolnshire and Selby to pick up the best piglets we can find.

I could go on. It's a funny thing, but get two pig farmers together and they'll talk about nothing else. We're just delighted we can go somewhere in Sheffield for a full English that's perfection on a plate.

Max Feetham

Everything but the oink!

Our love affair with pigs and their meat started thousands of years ago. The first domesticated pigs, probably related to wild boars, can be traced back to 5000 BC in the Near East and China. Their popularity spread thanks to the fact they were easy to keep, ate up scraps and most importantly every part of them could be eaten. Nowadays their meat is the most commonly consumed worldwide and features in different guises across global cuisine, from red roasted Asian pork to Italian pancetta and salamis, Spanish chorizo to our own bacon, sausages and roasts.

In England before the Industrial Revolution, almost every home would keep its own pig. It would be fattened up through spring and summer before being slaughtered and eaten throughout the autumn and winter. Pig by-products including lard and preserved meats like bacon, ham and gammon would be prepared through the cold months so a family could live off its pig for an entire year.

Commercial production and refrigeration mean that for the last century we've eaten pork throughout the year, but flavour and quality have suffered. Thankfully the tide is turning as more people are returning to traditional methods of pig rearing or even starting to keep pigs for the first time. In fact in the five years up to 2008, the number of smallholdings keeping fewer than ten fattening pigs rose by 32 percent. Rare breed pigs are enjoying a revival as, although they take longer to mature than breeds chosen for intensive, commercial farming, their meat is considered far superior.

In tandem with this, forgotten cuts have become more popular and once again diners can experience the unique tastes offered by different parts of the animal. We've had an adventure with our Nose to Tail weeks, which all started when we took delivery of the first pigs from our own herd. We want to share our journey of discovery that resulted in a new world of cooking – using everything but the oink!

Cuts of pork

Most of these cuts can be supplied by your local butcher. He'll also give you guidance on cooking times and methods. Try something new and surprise yourself:

HEAD: This can be delicious if cooked the right way. If you're not up for it yourself, ask your butcher to bone and tie the head before preparing it for slow cooking in a pot of stock. Also use for brawn, stocks and soups.

CHEEK: A beautifully tender cut of meat that has become a favourite in our kitchen.

EARS: So long consigned to use as dog treats, these are delicious fried and baked after boiling.

SHOULDER: Cubed shoulder pork is great for casseroles, stews and curries. For roasting, buy shoulder joint (which can be boned and rolled) and knuckle/shank for slow roasting; spare rib joint, mini collar joint and collar joint for roasting or slow cooking.

HAND: A less commonly known and cheaper cut of pork, which is good for burgers or slow braising.

LOIN: This cut from along the pig's back provides particularly fine joints (boned and rolled loin joint or loin rack joint) for roasting. A variety of steaks can be cut from the loin including: loin eye, Valentine steak (shaped like a heart) and loin steaks for frying or griddling.

BELLY: Pork belly loves marinades and stuffing prior to slow roasting. Cuts include rustic belly (with criss-cross scored fat) and rolled belly joints, large and mini belly slices and spare ribs.

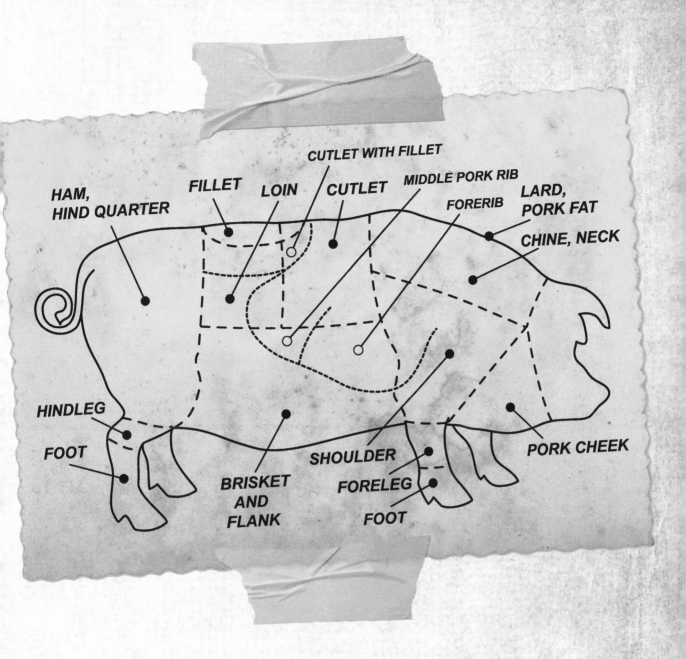

LEG: This provides the meatiest cuts. Leg joints and cushion leg joints are perfect for roasting with crispy crackling. Ham, leg steaks, and pork bucco also derive from the leg joint.

TENDERLOIN: A cut taken from the top of the back, this cut is renowned for its succulence and superb quality. Provides lean pieces for roasting whole or medallions for poaching and griddling.

CHUMP: Best known for providing chump steaks, this cut comes from where the back meets the leg. Also gives a fantastic joint to roast.

TROTTERS AND HOCKS: Usually cooked in soups or stews, this part of the pig is tasty and cheap to buy.

TAIL: Another forgotten part of the pig, the tail has long had a place in many world cuisines and is making a revival in British cooking.

LIVER, KIDNEY, HEART, TONGUE: Pork offal is incredibly delicious and features in a variety of dishes in The Milestone.

Fair game

To chefs, autumn is more about birds dropping from the sky than colourful leaves. This is the time when the shooting season begins in earnest and game from the nearby Peak District finds its way to The Milestone's kitchen. Not only is this bounty truly delicious, it's also free-range, organic, local and very fresh.

The aptly named Ben Fowler provides us with all our game requirements, from rabbit and wild duck to pheasant and woodpigeon.

All game is seasonal to an extent. Even birds you always see around like woodpigeon are agricultural pests and culled more at harvest time. Woodpigeon, as the name suggests, roost in trees and woodland, but fly into the open fields to feed on barley, oil seed, rape and wheat. Unlike their city-dwelling cousins, they enjoy a fabulous diet that makes them so tasty, but damages crops. From the end of July to the beginning of April we shoot them on their feeding grounds in farmers' fields using decoys like plastic and rubber pigeons, dead birds or sometimes a rocking cradle to create movement and attract live woodpigeons to them.

Like woodpigeon, pheasant live in woodland areas. They tend to keep undercover so the shoot uses a team of beaters and dogs to flush them into the open and drive them over 'the guns' outside the wood. We wait until we can see sky before shooting them high overhead, aiming between 10 and 2 on a clockface. Although the majority of pheasants are reared and released for shooting, there are some wild ones around in the countryside.

The season for wild duck or mallard is from September 1 to the end of January. These birds live on large lakes or reservoirs during the day, but fly to smaller ponds to feed and roost at dusk. We scatter barley around ponds and wait for the ducks to come, shooting them as they fly in. We also shoot mallard over farmers' fields, where they too can damage crops prior to the harvest. We only use non-toxic shots for duck to protect the waterways. All game birds are retrieved by our gundogs and placed on a game cart before being taken back and hung in fridges for up to 12 days for tenderising. In times gone by, game was hung by its neck until the body dropped off, but our modern stomachs probably couldn't cope with that!

We tend to ferret for rabbits from October 1 when they have stopped breeding, the young are big enough to be caught and the foliage is less dense, making it easier to spot their holes. We block the exits with nets and send ferrets into the warren complex, trapping them as they bolt. We don't shoot the rabbits, but dispatch them immediately. Some people send lurchers or greyhounds after rabbits, but that can only be effective in large areas of open land. On an average ferreting trip we will catch around 30 wild rabbits, ridding farmers of a nuisance and providing great meat for The Milestone. We don't catch hare locally, as there's such a small population here it wouldn't be sustainable; most hare comes from Lincolnshire.

Everything we hunt is sold to local restaurants or eaten ourselves, unlike the kill from big commercial or recreational shoots that often goes to waste.

In lots of ways shooting is a job that has to be done to help farmers. I've been shooting since I was 14 and I still love going out, whatever the weather. Sometimes I come back empty-handed and in that respect it's a little like fishing. The big difference is I can never lie about the size of the pigeon I shot.'

Ben Fowler

...with respect

At The Milestone, we look forward to the cornucopia of game arriving during the season. Wildfowl and rabbits are naturally active over large areas so their meat is very lean compared to commercially-reared animals that don't have to forage for food and have no natural predators.

When cooking game, we keep things as basic as possible so the distinctive taste of the meat can speak for itself. All the flavour is in the juices, so it is better cooked rare otherwise the tight protein can become liver-like and tough. We like to use sweet embellishments such as chocolate, fruits, root vegetables and legumes to counterbalance the succulent, earthy quality of the meat. We team duck with rhubarb, pigeon pie with peas, venison with chocolate or redcurrants and rabbit with carrot purée and braised lettuce.

We looked back through history for recipe ideas to when game was more commonly eaten. We have built an exciting repertoire of cooking methods for our special game weeks at the restaurant. We also use offal from game such as minced venison heart and rabbit liver. Not only are these cuts incredibly tasty, they cost a fraction of the price of the actual meat.

We run special game weeks throughout the shooting season, introducing our customers to a truly sumptuous riot of flavours. That said, even simple dishes like pigeon pie have become incredibly popular.

People find it hard to conceptualise how a feathery bird or furry rabbit can become a beautiful dish on the plate. That's because we've lost our connection with the journey produce makes from field to fork. It's something we keep alive at The Milestone, where respect for the seasons and our local riches is the foundation of our cooking.

Simon Ayres

Local Produce

The Milestone champions itself on working with suppliers to source ingredients that are as local as possible and to a high standard

Examples are -

Carrotts - Poskitts Farm Wakefield

Parsnips - Poskitts Farm Wakefield

New Potatoes - Holme Farm, Goldthorpe, Barnsley

Tomato - Williamsons - East Yorkshire

Herbs - Thirsk, North Yorkshire

English Onions - Harthill

Leeks, baby leeks, white, green spring cabbage
- Mutton Farm, Bolsover

Asparagus - English

Strawberries - English

Milk - Newfield Dairy Mansfield

Pick of the crop

Fresh potatoes forked from the earth, cabbages prised from the soil, berries picked from bushes and apples plucked from trees. Even if you've been growing vegetables for years, there's always something miraculous about harvesting your own food. All the backbreaking work it entails has a terrific pay-off: the fabulous taste of truly fresh fruit and veg. We do everything at The Milestone to deliver that pristine flavour on a plate. And where better to source our fruit and veg than from Sheffield's finest allotment growers?

We struck on the idea some time ago when one of our customers brought in a glut of his vegetables to see if we wanted them. Not only did we accept with delight, we wanted much more. Word got around and soon we were welcoming a parade of proud growers with their premium produce into our kitchen. Whatever's in season arrives very soon after it's cropped. Our aim is always to use the fruit and veg at its freshest and we work what we're given into our menu, even if that means altering a planned dish.

In Sheffield there are plenty of people who've worked on their allotments for decades. There are many more waiting for a little patch of earth. We were amazed to learn that waiting time for the most popular allotments can be as long as 10 years. This year there are 2,300 people on Sheffield Council's waiting list, hoping for one of the mere 3,000 plots to become available. To get more 'keen-beans' digging for dinner, the council has planned five new allotment sites and is making unscheduled spot checks to identify poorly-maintained plots, which tenants might have to hand back. So start straightening up!

The Milestone has a great relationship with allotment growers in the city, who bring us their surplus in exchange for vouchers for drinks, meals or the cookery school. We receive trays of soft fruit, bunches of rhubarb, sacks of potatoes, peas, cabbages and beans of every variety. Whatever comes in finds its way to the plate very quickly, so our diners can experience that 'just picked' taste. It's a perfect arrangement that provides The Milestone with organic, local produce and those hardworking gardeners with a bit of a treat.

Britain was a nation of gardeners long before it became a nation of shopkeepers. Subsistence farming was the way of life for our sealocked ancestors. The idea of nurturing fruit and vegetables for our own consumption has become a trendy ideology, but for many years allotments provided everything for the family table.

Allotments started thousands of years ago when the Saxons cleared woods to create common land for farming. After the Norman Conquest, feudal peasants worked strips of land for the lord. In the Elizabethan era, tenants who had been dispossessed of land for enclosure were given small allotments attached to their cottages in compensation.

In the Victorian era, allotments were made available to terrace-dwelling workers in major towns to keep people fed, occupied and out of the pubs.

During and after WW2, blockades and rationing kept the demand for homegrown food high. The number of UK allotments peaked at almost 1.5 million, but steadily declined until a revival of interest in the 70s. This was in part due to TV sit-com 'The Good Life' which made viewers yearn for the self-sufficient idyll portrayed by Tom and Barbara (Richard Briers and Felicity Kendall). The programme was years ahead of its time and is still credited with inspiring many fans to start growing their own.

Demand for allotments levelled off in the 80s and 90s, then began to rise as more city-slickers resolved to cultivate their own little patch and grow 'real food'. Even the Queen recently turned over part of the palace grounds to growing fruit and vegetables for the first time since the war. Her Majesty's has some celebrity company; Jamie Oliver, Charles Dance and Radio 4's John Humphreys all keep allotments too.

James Wallis

Beetroot and vodka pickled herring, a dill Martini, beetroot salad and horseradish crème fraîche

Ingredients

FOR THE HERRING:

4 fillets herring

100ml vodka

200g raw beetroot, grated

150ml white wine vinegar

100g caster sugar

1 teaspoon coriander seeds

1 teaspoon fennel seeds

150g Maldon sea salt

TO MAKE A BEETROOT SALAD:

2 beetroots (we use candy stripe and yellow)

FOR HORSERADISH CRÈME FRAÎCHE

100g crème fraîche

1 tablespoon horseradish sauce

Juice of half a lemon

TO MAKE A DILL MARTINI:

75ml Noilly Prat

75ml vodka

Large handful dill

Juice 1 lemon

25ml sugar syrup (made from equal quantities of sugar and water brought to the boil and then simmered until thickened slightly)

Method

For the herring:

Ensure the herring is free from any pinbones and then place on a plastic tray with the Maldon sea salt covering it. Cover with cling film and place in the fridge for 3 hours to help cure and firm up the fish.

Wash off the salt under cold running water and then pat dry with kitchen roll.

To make the pickle, place the vodka, caster sugar, vinegar, coriander seeds and fennel seeds in a saucepan and then bring to the boil. Allow to cool and add the grated beetroot.

Blend in a liquidiser into a fine purée.

Place the herring in the cool pickle and allow to cure for 24 hours.

Remove the herring from the pickle and then pat dry with kitchen roll. Slice each fillet into three portions and reserve for plating.

For the beetroot salad:

Cook the beetroot, boil in their skins until soft. Peel and then cut into 1cm cubes.

To make the horseradish crème fraîche:

Mix all the ingredients together and leave to infuse for an hour, then pass through a fine sieve.

Dill Martini:

Add all the ingredients into a cocktail shaker with ice and then shake for 10 seconds, strain and discard the ice and dill.

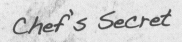

Chef's Secret

Make sure you use raw uncooked beetroot for the herring, otherwise you will not achieve the brilliant magenta colour.

Black pudding, home cured bacon, fried quail's egg and Bloody Mary

Ingredients

Quail eggs, one per person

FOR THE BLACK PUDDING:

1 litre fresh pig's blood

1 onion, finely chopped

1 clove garlic

12 sage leaves, finely chopped

125g pork back fat, cut into 1cm cubes

75g sultanas

75g pearl barley, boiled until soft

75g porridge oats

Pinch white pepper

FOR THE BACON:

1 pork belly rib, bones removed

500g sea salt

250g caster sugar

2 star anise, crushed

5 cloves

FOR THE BLOODY MARY:

50ml vodka

200ml tomato juice

Pinch salt and pepper

2 dashes tabasco

Half a lemon, juiced

Method

To make the black pudding:

Blend the blood with a stick blender until smooth.

Pass through a fine sieve.

Cook the onion, garlic and sage until soft.

Add the remaining ingredients and cook over a low heat for 10-15 minutes.

Place the mix in a terrine mould lined with baking parchment and bake in a bain marie at 120ºc for 45 minutes.

Check the black pudding is cooked by placing a knife into the centre of the pudding. If clean, the pudding is cooked.

Remove from the oven and allow to cool.

To cure the bacon:

Mix ingredients and rub onto the pork.

Place on a plastic tray.

Cover and refrigerate for 5 days.

Wash the curing mixture off the meat and pat dry.

Slice with a meat slicer or sharp knife.

Lay the rashers on a flat baking tray, place another tray on top and bake at 170ºc for 5-10 minutes until crisp.

For the Bloody Mary:

Mix ingredients with ice and strain.

Serve in shot glasses.

To assemble:

Pan-fry the quail eggs.

Pan-fry the black pudding in a little oil and top with the egg and bacon.

Serve with the Bloody Mary.

Butternut squash and orange risotto

Ingredients

200g risotto rice (we use Arborio)

Half litre vegetable stock, (hot)

1 large butternut squash

1 small bunch of parsley, finely chopped

1 small bunch of tarragon, finely chopped

1 small onion, finely diced

85g Parmesan

50g butter

1 large orange

Method

To make the butternut purée:

Wrap the butternut squash in tinfoil and roast at 170ºc for 1 hour.

Remove from the oven and allow to cool. Cut in half and remove seeds.

Scoop out the flesh and discard the skin and the seeds.

Place the flesh in a food processor with 25g of the butter and blend to a smooth purée.

Reserve until finishing the risotto.

For the risotto:

In a pan large enough to cook the rice, sweat the onions in a small amount of vegetable oil until soft and translucent.

Stir in the rice ensuring you coat all the grains. Pour on the white wine and reduce until almost disappeared, then cover with 2 ladles of the vegetable stock.

Cook until nearly absorbed and repeat until all the stock is gone and the rice is al dente.

Stir through the purée (you will probably need only half or so), and add the orange segments, Parmesan and butter. Season with salt and serve.

Curried cauliflower soup

Ingredients

2 heads cauliflower, cut into florets

1 onion, peeled and chopped

2 cloves garlic

1 teaspoon mild curry paste

1 teaspoon garam masala

2 pints milk

1 red chilli, chopped and de-seeded

Method

Cook the onion, garlic, curry paste, chilli and garam masala in a teaspoon of oil until soft.

Pour in the milk and bring to the boil.

Add the cauliflower and simmer for 10 minutes.

Place in a liquidiser and blend to a fine purée.

Season with salt and pass through a sieve.

Ideal served with fresh homemade bread, see our recipe on page 159.

Milestone fish fingers in beer batter

Ingredients

FOR THE FISH FINGERS:

400g white fish, cut into fingers
(Pollock, Coley or Cod are ideal)

FOR THE BATTER:

200g plain flour

350g beer

100g cornflour

1 egg yolk

FOR THE MUSHY PEAS:

200g frozen peas

50g butter

Handful of mint leaves

Method

For the fish fingers:

First roll the fish in the flour, then the egg and finally the breadcrumbs.

Deep fry at 180°c for 4-5 minutes or until golden and the fish is cooked through.

To make the mushy peas:

Blanch the peas for 30 seconds in a pan of boiling water and then place into a food processor.

Add the butter and mint and pulse until a thickish consistency.

Serve with a wedge of lemon and some tartar sauce.

Chef's Secret

Perfect comfort food. Everyone's favourite and guaranteed no added e-numbers or minced up fish trimmings!

It's the reel thing

Fishing

Red mullet terrine with wasabi mayonnaise and caper dressing

Ingredients

1kg fresh red mullet fillets, pin boned and descaled

1 leek (use only the white part)

FOR THE DRESSING:

30g caperberries in brine

50ml olive oil

Juice of 1 lemon

Handful of finely chopped parsley

FOR THE WASABI MAYONNAISE:

2 medium egg yolks

25ml white wine vinegar

1 teaspoon wasabi paste

300ml light olive oil

Good squeeze fresh lemon juice

1 teaspoon lecithin powder

1 tablespoon water

Method

Cut the root off the leek and then thoroughly wash the leek in cold water.

Place the leek in a large pan of boiling water for 10 seconds to soften and then place in cold iced water to refresh and stop cooking.

Gently pan-fry the mullet in a small amount of oil until cooked through.

Line a terrine mould with cling film and then add a layer of the leeks. Allow a small amount of overlap on the cling film to finish the terrine.

Fill the terrine with the mullet and then seal the cling film.

Place a heavy weight on top of the terrine and press in the fridge for 24 hours.

Once set, cut into 1.5cm slices. Take great care in doing this as the terrine is quite delicate.

How to make the mayonnaise:

Sit a large bowl on a cloth to stop it moving.

Put the egg yolks, vinegar and lecithin into the bowl and whisk well until smooth.

Tip: You can also make this in a food processor, adding the oil through the feeder tube. It will keep in the fridge for 3-4 days.

Gradually add the olive oil in a slow, steady stream, whisking all the time. You should have a smooth, quite thick mayonnaise that stands in peaks.

Add the water and wasabi paste then add the lemon juice to taste and briefly whisk.

For the dressing:

Drain the capers from the brine and pan-fry until crisp then mix all the remaining ingredients together.

This is a really great way to enjoy fresh fish. If you prefer you can swap the wasabi mayonnaise for horseradish mayonnaise.

Ox tongue fritters & sweet chilli jam

Don't let the cat get your tongue! This dish isn't as daunting in preparation as you might think, and the rich, robust flavour of the meat is well worth it.

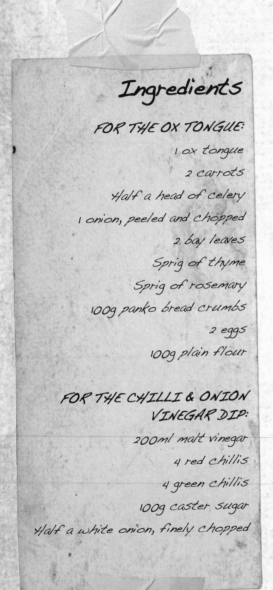

Ingredients

FOR THE OX TONGUE:

1 ox tongue

2 carrots

Half a head of celery

1 onion, peeled and chopped

2 bay leaves

Sprig of thyme

Sprig of rosemary

100g panko bread crumbs

2 eggs

100g plain flour

FOR THE CHILLI & ONION VINEGAR DIP:

200ml malt vinegar

4 red chillis

4 green chillis

100g caster sugar

Half a white onion, finely chopped

Method

For the ox tongue:

Place the ox tongue in cold water and bring to the boil. Once it starts to boil, refresh under cold running water.

Repeat the process once more. This removes any scum and bitterness from the ox tongue.

On the third boil add all the vegetables and aromatics, then simmer for three hours until the ox tongue is tender.

Remove from the liquid. When it is cool enough to handle peel away the tough outer layer of the tongue.

Chop the tongue into cubes and place through a meat mincer. If you do not have one put it through a food processor and the texture will still be acceptable.

Place the tongue mince into a tray lined with parchment, place another sheet on top and then weigh down with another tray. Press down firmly and leave to set in the fridge.

Once set, cut into 1 inch cubes ready for the crumbs.

To breadcrumb the meat, roll the cubes through the flour, then the beaten egg and then the panko breadcrumbs.

Deep fry at 180ºc until golden and crisp.

For the chilli dip:

Place all the ingredients in a saucepan and boil until reduced by half. Allow to cool and serve with the fritters.

Chef's Secret

Try to get Japanese panko breadcrumbs, they're made from bread without crusts, and have a crisper texture than normal breadcrumbs.

Pea pannacotta, shoots, seeds, soil and flowers

Ingredients

FOR THE PANNACOTTA:

400g peas

2g agar agar powder (if not vegetarian gelatine can be substituted use 4 leaves soaked in cold water)

FOR THE SOIL:

200g black olives

Tablespoon of water

FOR THE GARNISH:

Handful pea shoots

25g mixed seeds (we use sesame, sunflower and linseed)

25g sprouting shoots

Small handful of edible flowers i.e nasturtiums, pansies, rose or violet

Method

To make the pannacotta:

Bring a large pan of water to the boil and blanch the peas until soft. Blend the peas with a small amount of the cooking liquor and then pass though a fine strainer.

Add a small amount of the cooking liquor until you have a pint of purée.

Chill in a metal bowl over another bowl filled with ice. This cools the purée quickly and retains the bright green colour.

Season with salt to taste.

Bring a small amount of the liquid to the boil and whisk in the agar agar powder, add the remaining pea purée and then set in dariole moulds in the fridge.

To turn out, dip the mould into boiling water for 1 second to loosen the pannacotta.

For the soil:

Place the black olives in a blender with a tablespoon of water and blend to a smooth purée.

To assemble:

Place the pannacotta on the plate and make a 'path' with the seeds. Spread the 'soil' on the plate, and scatter a few pea shoots around.

61

Pigeon black pudding salad with sloe gin dressing

Ingredients

4 pigeon breasts

100g watercress

FOR THE BLACK PUDDING:

1 litre fresh pig's blood

1 onion, finely chopped

1 clove garlic

12 sage leaves, finely chopped

125g pork back fat, cut into 1cm cubes

75g sultanas

75g pearl barley, boiled until soft

75g porridge oats

Pinch white pepper

SLOE GIN DRESSING:

1 egg yolk

100ml vegetable oil

30ml white wine vinegar

25ml sloe gin

2 juniper berries, ground to a powder

Pinch of salt

Method

For the dressing:

Whisk the egg yolk and vinegar until light, fluffy and doubled in size.

Slowly pour in the vegetable oil, whisking at all times so the dressing does not split.

Repeat the process with the sloe gin, then add the ground juniper berries.

Season with salt.

To make the black pudding:

Blend the blood with a stick blender until smooth.

Pass through a fine sieve.

Cook the onion, garlic and sage until soft.

Add the remaining ingredients and cook over a low heat for 10-15 minutes.

Place the mix in a terrine mould lined with baking parchment and bake in a bain marie at 120°c for 45 minutes.

Check the black pudding is cooked by placing a knife into the centre of the pudding. If clean, the pudding is cooked.

Remove from the oven and allow to cool.

To assemble:

Pan-fry the pigeon breast and the black pudding (we serve the pigeon pink but cook according to your own preference).

Toss the spinach leaves in a small amount of the dressing.

Place the salad in a bowl, top with the a slice of black pudding and then the pigeon.

Drizzle the remaining dressing over the pigeon and serve.

Pigeon pudding and pea purée

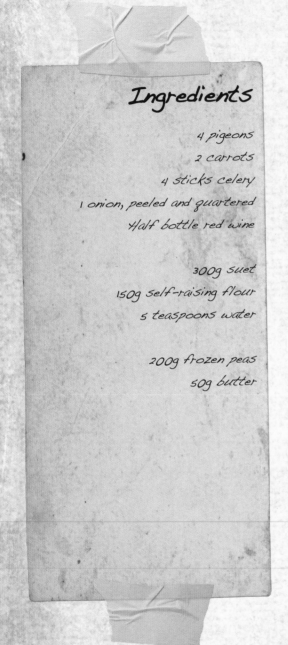

Ingredients

4 pigeons
2 carrots
4 sticks celery
1 onion, peeled and quartered
Half bottle red wine

300g suet
150g self-raising flour
5 teaspoons water

200g frozen peas
50g butter

Method

For the pigeons:

In a hot pan, colour the pigeons all over with a small amount of vegetable oil. Remove from the pan and set aside. Add the vegetables and colour. Pour in the red wine and reduce by two thirds.

Place the pigeons and vegtables in a deep ovenproof dish. Cover with cold water then seal with tin foil and place in a pre-heated oven at 140ºc. Braise for 3 hours.

Once tender, remove the pigeons from the liquor and leave until cool enough to handle. Pick all the meat from the birds, ensuring no bones remain. Pass the cooking liquor through a fine sieve, skim the stock of any fat and scum and reduce to an intensely-flavoured sauce. Combine the sauce and the shredded pigeon meat.

To make the suet paste:

Sieve the flour into a large electric mixing bowl. Add the suet and water and mix on a medium speed until the fat is incorporated into the flour and a smooth dough is formed. Allow the dough to rest in the fridge for 30 minutes.

For the pea purée:

Blanch the peas in a large pan of salted boiling water, then place in a liquidiser and blend until smooth. Add the butter to help emulsify and then pass through a fine sieve. Season with salt and set aside.

To make the puddings:

Lightly coat the inside of small dariole moulds or steamproof earthenware dishes with butter. Roll out the pastry to the thickness of a pound coin and then line the moulds. Spoon in the filling. When almost full, place another disc of the pastry on top and seal with water.

Place the puddings in a steamer for 45 minutes - 1 hour. Turn out the puddings immediately and serve with the heated pea purée.

Home cured bacon, asparagus and poached quail eggs, truffle vinagrette

Serves 4

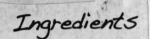

Ingredients

16 asparagus spears

12 quails' eggs

TO MAKE YOUR OWN BACON:

Half a pork belly

500g Maldon sea salt

250g caster sugar

3 cloves

1 cinnamon stick broken up

3 star anise

10 juniper berries

FOR THE MAYONNAISE:

2 medium egg yolks

25ml white wine vinegar

1 teaspoon truffle oil

300ml light olive oil

Good squeeze fresh lemon juice

1 teaspoon lecithin powder

1 tablespoon water

Method

First make the bacon in advance:

Mix all the ingredients together and then rub into the pork belly. Place on a plastic tray and then cling film tightly and refrigerate for 4 days minimum and 6 maximum, we find 5 ideal.

After 4-6 days, wash the bacon in cold water and then pat dry with kitchen roll and then freeze for two hours to firm up.

How to make the mayonnaise:

Sit a large bowl on a cloth to stop it moving.

Put the egg yolks, vinegar and lecithin into the bowl and whisk well until smooth.

Tip: You can also make this in a food processor, adding the oil through the feeder tube. It will keep in the fridge for 3-4 days.

Gradually add the olive oil in a slow, steady stream, whisking all the time. You should have a smooth, quite thick mayonnaise that stands in peaks.

Add the water and truffle oil and add lemon juice to taste then briefly whisk.

To poach the quails eggs:

Bring a pan of water to the boil and add a good splash of white wine vinegar.

Crack the quails eggs into small ramekins and discard any that have split yolks, poach for 1 minute and then refresh into cold water.

Snap the asparagus at the woody points and then peel the stems, blanch in boiling water for 20-30 seconds or until tender, then place in iced water to stop the cooking.

To make the bacon crisps:

Slice the bacon as thin as possible and then place between two layers of parchment and between two heavy baking trays, bake at 170°c for 10-15 minutes until crisp.

To assemble:

Reheat the asparagus and quails egg in a pan of boiling water.

Place the spears on the bottom of the plate and then pour on some of the dressing. Top the asparagus with the eggs and the bacon crisps and garnish with pea shoots.

Chef's Secret

This dish is best enjoyed in the six short weeks that British asparagus is in season - a real treat, enjoy it while you can.

Salmon cured in botanicals with a cucumber, lime and Hendricks gin chilled soup

Ingredients

Half a side salmon
250g Maldon seasalt
125g caster sugar
6 juniper berries
18 coriander seeds
1 small piece of cassia bark
Quarter stick of liquorice, grated
2 lemons, zested

FOR THE CUCUMBER SOUP:

2 cucumbers, peeled and seeds removed
100ml tonic water
75ml Hendricks gin
25ml sugar syrup (equal quantities of sugar and water cooked out until slightly thickened)
Small handful of coriander leaves
Small handful of mint leaves
Juice of 1 lime

Method

To cure the salmon:

Mix all the ingredients together and then rub into the salmon. Allow to cure in the fridge, wrapped tightly in cling film, for 12 hours.

Wash the salmon in cold water and then pat dry with kitchen roll. Slice thinly (to a similar thickness to smoked salmon) and remove the dark brown meat, as this tends to be quite bitter.

For the cucumber soup:

Place all the ingredients in a liquidiser and blend until smooth. Pass through a fine sieve and season with salt.

To serve:

Place some of the salmon in a bowl and add the soup, float a few borage flowers in the soup (borage flowers are purple and have a cucumber flavour).

Chef's Secret

This is a cheffy take on a gin & tonic.
Hendricks gin is made with cucumbers and salmon has a natural affinity.
A very English cooling summer dish.

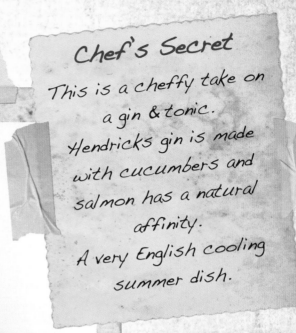

Hop cured salmon with local real ale

Ingredients

Half side of salmon

250g Maldon sea salt

50ml dark treacle

125g caster sugar

15g dried hops

Method

To cure the salmon:

Mix all the ingredients together and then rub into the salmon. Allow to cure in the fridge, wrapped tightly in cling film, for 12 hours.

Wash the salmon in cold water and then pat dry with kitchen roll. Slice thinly (to a similar thickness to smoked salmon) and remove the dark brown meat, as this tends to be quite bitter.

To serve:

With half a glass of Kelham Island Best Bitter but if you fancy a full pint with it… well, why not?

The hops are the perfect bitter counter balance for the rich and salty salmon.

You can buy hops from any good brewers shop, or from the internet

Cured sea trout with rocket purée

Chef's Secret

The creaminess of the sea trout benefits from the peppery tang of the rocket.

Ingredients

One side of line caught sea trout

250g Maldon sea salt

125g caster sugar

100g rocket

Method

To cure the sea trout, mix all the ingredients together except the rocket and then rub into the sea trout.

Wrap the trout tightly in cling film and allow to cure in the fridge for 12 hours.

Wash the sea trout in cold water and then pat dry with kitchen roll.

Bring a large pan of water to the boil and blanch the rocket for 8 seconds to wilt it. Drain and then purée in a liquidiser. Once cool, rub all the rocket over the sea trout.

Slice thinly to a thickness of 1-2cm and remove the dark brown meat as this tends to be quite bitter.

Serve with a spoonfull of the purée and a fresh cucumber salad.

Pan-fried scallops, carpaccio of pigs head, squid and squid ink

Ingredients

4 scallops

4 baby squid tubes, cut into thin strips

Handful pea shoots (to garnish)

FOR THE PIG'S HEAD:

1 pig's head

2 carrots, peeled and chopped

4 sticks celery, peeled and chopped

1 star anise

1 onion, peeled and chopped

1 white leek

Half bottle white wine

2 cloves garlic

Water to cover

FOR THE SQUID INK PAINT:

5g squid ink

15ml vegetable oil

Method

To prepare the pig's head:

To bone the head, run a boning knife from the top of the skull, following the line of the bone closely to avoid breaking the skin.

Remove the flesh from the right hand cheek and repeat on the left.

Cut off the ears and remove any hairs with a razor or blowtorch.

Butterfly the cheek meat, cut the tongue in half and place each half in each side of the head.

Season with salt and roll tightly in cling film to maintain the shape.

Place the remaining ingredients in an ovenproof dish with a tight-fitting lid and cover with water.

Braise at 140ºc for 4-5 hours, until tender.

Remove the head from the cooking juices and allow to cool. When cool enough to handle, remove the cling film and then re-roll in more cling film, ensuring it is watertight.

Place in an ice bath to cool.

To assemble:

Whisk the squid ink and oil together.

Fry the squid over a high heat for 30 seconds.

Pan-fry the scallops for 45 seconds on each side.

Using a sharp knife, cut a thin slice of the pig's head and place on a warm plate.

Paint the squid ink onto the plate using a pastry brush, place the squid and scallops on the slice of pig's head and garnish with a few pea shoots.

Pan-fried scallop, ox tongue corn beef and tomato fondue

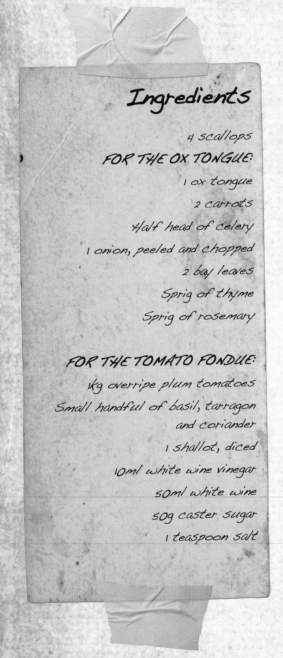

Ingredients

4 scallops

FOR THE OX TONGUE:

1 ox tongue

2 carrots

Half head of celery

1 onion, peeled and chopped

2 bay leaves

Sprig of thyme

Sprig of rosemary

FOR THE TOMATO FONDUE:

1kg overripe plum tomatoes

Small handful of basil, tarragon and coriander

1 shallot, diced

10ml white wine vinegar

50ml white wine

50g caster sugar

1 teaspoon salt

Method

For the scallops:

To remove the scallops from the shells, hold the shell open with your thumb and grip the back with your fingers. Scrape a butter knife along the flat side to release the scallop from the shell.

Remove the roe, black sac and beard from the scallop and then wash and pat dry with kitchen roll.

To make the ox tongue:

Place the ox tongue in colt water and bring to the boil. Once it starts to boil, refresh under cold running water

Repeat the process once more. This removes any scum and bitterness from the tongue

On the third boil add all the vegetables and aromatics. Simmer for 3 hours until the tongue is soft

Remove from the liquor and peel away the tough outer layer when it is cool enough to handle

Once cool, chop the tongue into cubes and place through a meat mincer. If you do not have one, put it through a food processor and the texture will still be acceptable

Place the tongue mince into a tray lined with parchment. Place another sheet on top and then another tray. Press down firmly and set in the fridge

To make the tomato fondue:

First ensure sure all equipment is particularly clean and well sanitised.

Core the tomatoes and cut into quarters.

Combine all the ingredients and leave to infuse for 3 hours.

Purée in a blender until smooth.

To assemble:

Place the ox tongue into a circle cutter and flatten.

Pan-fry the scallops for 1-2 minutes on each side.

Top the corned beef with the fondue and place the scallop on top.

Scallops with a citrus butter and lobster mayonnaise

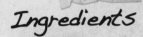

Ingredients

12 large scallops

1 small lobster

Small handful pea shoots to garnish

FOR THE LOBSTER REDUCTION:

Reserved lobster shells

50g each of carrots, celery and onion, diced

150ml tomato juice

1-2 bay leaves

100ml white wine

50ml Noilly Prat

300ml water

FOR THE CITRUS BUTTER:

50g unsalted butter

Zest of 1 lemon and juice

FOR THE LOBSTER MAYONNAISE:

2 medium egg yolks

1 teaspoon Dijon mustard

300ml light olive oil

Squeeze fresh lemon juice

Pinch salt and pepper

Method

For the lobster:

To humanely dispatch the lobster, place in the freezer an hour before cooking. This will send the lobster to sleep by slowing its nervous system down.

Bring a large pan of salted water to the boil. Place the lobster in the water and cook for 8 minutes. Plunge into a large pan of cold iced water to immediately stop the cooking.

Remove the claws and using either a lobster cracker or the back of a heavy knife, break the claws and pick out the meat. Split the lobster in two and remove the meat from the tail then clean out the head. Reserve the shells for the lobster reduction and the meat for the mayonnaise.

For the reduction:

Place the lobster shells into a roasting tray and then roast at 190ºc for 15 minutes. Blend the lobster meat in a food processor till the meat resembles fine grains.

Meanwhile sweat the celery, onion and carrots with a teaspoon of vegetable oil. Cook until soft.

Add the wine and Noilly Prat and then reduce until almost all the liquid has cooked off.

Add the lobster shells, tomato juice and water and simmer for 1 hour.

Place the mixture (shells included) into a liquidiser and blend until really smooth.

Pass the mixture through a fine strainer and then reduce over a medium heat until 100ml is left.

For the lobster mayonnaise:

Place the egg yolks into the bowl with the Dijon mustard and a little seasoning. Whisk until smooth.

Gradually add the olive oil in a slow, steady stream, whisking constantly. You should have a smooth, thick mayonnaise that stands in peaks.

Add lemon juice to taste.

If it's too thick, whisk in a few drops of warm water to give a good consistency.

Add the chopped lobster meat and the lobster reduction and gently whisk through.

To cook the scallops:

To remove the scallops from the shells, hold the shell open with your thumb and grip the back with your fingers. Scrape a butter knife along the flat side to release the scallop from the shell.

Remove the roe, black sac and beard from the scallop and then wash and pat dry with kitchen roll.

For the citrus butter:

Place the butter, zest and juice in a food processor and cream together. Place the butter in the fridge till ready for use.

To assemble:

Pan-fry the scallops in a hot pan for a minute or two on either side and then add the butter to the pan to coat the scallops.

Place three dollops of the mayonnaise on a plate and drag a line using the back of a spoon. Place the 3 scallops on the 3 lines of mayonnaise, pour over the butter and garnish with the pea shoots.

Sesame cured pollock with bok choi, sesame seeds and chilli salad

Ingredients

TO CURE THE POLLOCK:

400g pollock, scaled and pinboned

10ml sesame oil

200g sea salt

150g caster sugar

20g sesame seeds to garnish

FOR THE SALAD:

1 bok choi

Half red chilli, de-seeded

1 teaspoon sesame oil

1 teaspoon soy sauce

Method

To prepare the pollock:

Cover the pollock with the sesame oil, sugar and salt.

Wrap tightly in cling film and refrigerate for 4 hours.

Rinse off in cold running water and pat dry.

Rub the fish with the sesame seeds and slice wafer thin.

To make the salad:

Finely shred the bok choi and chilli and dress with sesame oil and soy sauce.

To assemble:

Lay the pollock onto a plate and top with the bok choi salad.

Drizzle the dressing around the plate.

Chef's Secret

Pollock is a great sustainable option instead of cod. If pollock is not available why not try mackerel or grey mullet.

Tomato consommé with edible soil, flowers and tomato agar

Ingredients

FOR THE CONSOMMÉ:

2kg overripe plum tomatoes

Small handful of basil, tarragon and coriander

1 shallot, diced

10ml white wine vinegar

50ml white wine

50g caster suger

1 teaspoon salt

FOR THE SOIL:

200g black olives

Tablespoon of water

FOR THE TOMATO AGAR:

200g tomato consommé

1g agar agar

TO GARNISH:

Pea shoots

Edible flowers

Method

For the consommé:

First ensure all equipment is particularly clean and well-sanitised.

Core the tomatoes and cut into quarters.

Combine all the ingredients and leave to infuse for 3 hours.

Purée in a blender until smooth.

Hang the pulp in a muslin bag and transfer to a cool place then allow the clear consommé to drip through into a container for 24 hours.

Bring the clear consommé to the boil and then correct the seasoning.

For the soil:

Place the black olives in a blender with a tablespoon of water and blend to a smooth purée.

To make the tomato agar:

Place the 200g consommé in a saucepan and bring to the boil.

Whisk in the agar agar powder and keeping whisking until fully disolved.

Pour into a small plastic container so the jelly will be 1cm thick when cut and set in the fridge.

To assemble:

Place a small plant pot or ramekin in the centre of the bowl and add your edible soil and decorative flowers.

Cut out 1cm cubes of the tomato agar agar jelly and place around the pot, then gently pour in a serving of the tomato consommé.

Chef's Secret

We serve our consommé
with a plant pot and
miniature watering can!

In hommage to
greenhouses full of ripe
summer tomatoes!

Yorkshire rarebit & Milestone Bread with Henderson's Relish

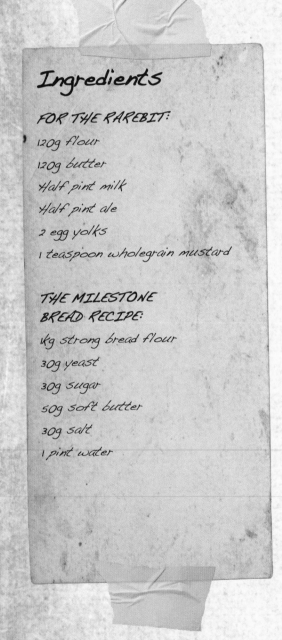

Ingredients

FOR THE RAREBIT:

120g flour

120g butter

Half pint milk

Half pint ale

2 egg yolks

1 teaspoon wholegrain mustard

THE MILESTONE BREAD RECIPE:

1kg strong bread flour

30g yeast

30g sugar

50g soft butter

30g salt

1 pint water

Method

To make the rarebit:

Melt the butter in a saucepan and add the flour, stir until mixed together into a roux.

Slowly add the milk and then bring to the boil.

After all the milk is stirred in, add the ale and cook out to a thick sauce.

Take off the heat and stir in the yolks and wholegrain mustard.

Season with salt and pepper to taste.

To finish slice 4 thick slices of bread (recipe below) and toast lightly.

Top with the rarebit and place under the grill until golden.

To bake your own Milestone Bread:

Combine the sugar, yeast, and water, then put to one side in a warm place and leave for 15 minutes.

Meanwhile, fold together the flour and salt and place in a food processor. If kneading by hand, tip the flour onto a work surface and make a well in the centre.

Add the liquid mix and the butter to the well and then mix until an elastic dough is formed.

Kneading by hand will take 10-15 minutes, if using a mixer about 5 minutes.

Cover with a clean damp cloth and then leave to prove in a warm place for 45 minutes-1 hour 30 minutes or until the dough has doubled in size.

Knead for another 5 minutes.

Cut into 2 large and 1 small loaves or into 3 for medium sized loaves.

Prove the loaves again until doubled in size.

Bake at 185°c for 25-35 minutes.

Chef's Secret

If you're from Sheffield then no further explanation will be required when we list Henderson's among the ingredients. For the benefit of those who are not so fortunate, it's a savoury sauce, a bit like Worcester Sauce - only better. This is a great supper dish, made all the more enjoyable by the satisfaction of having made your own bread.

Confit pork belly with black pudding, mashed potato and apple sauce

Ingredients

1kg pork belly
500g Duck or goose fat

FOR THE MASHED POTATO:

1kg desiree potatoes
100ml double cream
100ml semi-skimmed milk
150g butter
Few sprigs thyme
Few sprigs rosemary
Pinch of nutmeg
Pinch of white pepper

APPLE SAUCE:

2 Granny Smith apples
50g caster sugar
Juice 1 lemon
Seeds from half a vanilla pod
50ml water
50g butter

FOR THE BLACK PUDDING:

1 litre fresh pig's blood
1 onion, finely chopped
1 clove garlic
12 sage leaves, finely chopped
125g pork back fat, cut into 1cm cubes
75g sultanas
75g pearl barley, boiled until soft
75g porridge oats
Pinch white pepper

Method

To prepare the pork belly:

Warm the goose fat in a pan.

Place the pork belly in an ovenproof dish and cover with the fat.

Cover with tin foil and place in the oven at 120°c for 3 hours 30 minutes-4 hours.

To test whether the pork is cooked, cut into the meat with a knife. If it cuts through with little resistance it is cooked.

Remove from the oven and allow to cool.

Take the pork from the fat and place between 2 flat baking trays.

Wrap the trays tightly in cling film and place a heavy weight on top, to compress for 24 hours.

Cut 4 square portions, remove the skin and fry fat side down until crisp.

To make the mashed potato:

Peel the potatoes, season with salt and boil until soft.

Infuse the cream, milk and butter, with the thyme and rosemary in a pan for 15 minutes.

Drain the potatoes in a colander and allow to steam for 2 minutes.

Mash the potatoes with a potato ricer.

Sieve the cream and milk mix and beat into the mashed potato until light and fluffy.

Season with salt, pepper and nutmeg.

For the apple sauce:

Peel and core the apple and chop into inch cubes.

Place all the ingredients except the butter in a pan and cook until soft.

Liquidise the apples and butter until smooth.

Pass through a fine sieve.

To make the black pudding:

Blend the blood with a stick blender until smooth.

Pass through a fine sieve.

Cook the onion, garlic and sage until soft and combine with the blood.

Add the remaining ingredients and cook over a low heat for 10-15 minutes.

Place the mix in a terrine mould lined with baking parchment and bake in a bain marie at 120°c for 45 minutes.

Check the black pudding is cooked by placing a knife into the centre of the pudding. If clean, the pudding is cooked.

Remove from the oven and allow to cool.

Chef's Secret

We garnish this with crispy crackling - to make your crackling press the pig skin between two flat baking trays and bake until crispy.

Double eggs Benedict

Ingredients

8 rashers of home-cured bacon, grilled

8 poached eggs

200g spinach, wilted

FOR THE HOLLANDAISE SAUCE:

250g butter, melted and milk solids discarded

4 egg yolks

50ml white wine vinegar

Juice of half a lemon

Pinch of salt

TO MAKE THE MUFFINS:

500g bread flour

100g butter

Half pint of milk

15g fresh yeast

15g sugar

15g salt

Chef's Secret

This makes the perfect hangover cure, if you don't fancy making it on a hangover then get yourself over to The Milestone and have it made for you!

Method

For the hollandaise:

Mix the yolks and vinegar in a metal bowl and then whisk in a bain-marie until light, fluffy and doubled in size.

Slowly pour in the melted butter, whisking continuously until all is incorporated. Season with salt and lemon. Keep in a warm place until ready to serve.

To make the muffins:

Warm the milk to 37ºc and then whisk in the yeast, sugar and butter.

Add the salt to the flour and then mix all the ingredients together. Knead for 10 minutes. Cover the dough with a damp cloth and leave in a warm place to prove until doubled in size.

Remove and knead again for 5 minutes.

Weigh the muffins into 70g portions. Roll between your hands into neat balls. Allow to prove until almost doubled in size and then flatten the balls slightly and bake at 180ºc for 10-15 minutes.

To assemble:

Top the muffins with the spinach, followed by the bacon, poached eggs and finally the hollandaise.

Duck hot pot layered with sweet potatoes

Ingredients

TO COOK THE DUCK LEGS:

5 duck legs

250g duck or goose fat

FOR THE HOT POT:

Large handful of parsley, finely chopped

2 carrots

2 sticks of celery

1 leek (white part only)

100ml reduced veal stock

1 sweet potato

50g Parmesan

10g butter

Method

To cook the duck:

First, slowly melt the duck/goose fat.

Place the duck legs in an ovenproof dish and carefully pour over the melted fat.

Place in the oven at 130ºc for 2-2 hours 30 minutes. The duck should be falling off the bone and tender.

Remove the duck legs from the fat and allow to drain. Save the duck fat to use again.

Pick all the meat off the legs and discard the skin and bones.

For the hot pot:

Finely chop the carrot, celery and leek and then sweat in a little butter until soft but without colour.

Add the shredded duck meat, chopped parsley and veal stock.

Peel the sweet potato and slice thinly as you would for a potato hotpot.

Blanch in boiling salted water for 30 seconds to soften slightly.

Place the duck mix in pie dishes and then top with the sweet potato. Sprinkle over the grated parmesan.

Bake at 170ºc until hot and golden brown.

Fish pie with pipérade

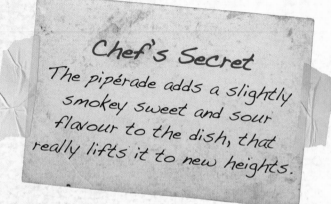

Ingredients

FOR THE PIPÉRADE:

4 red peppers, peeled and finely sliced

1 onion, finely sliced

Half teaspoon smoked paprika

1 clove of garlic

10ml sherry vinegar

FOR THE FISH PIE:

400g mashed potato

50g grated parmesan

700g diced mixed fish (smoked haddock, salmon and whiting is a good mix)

FOR THE BECHAMEL SAUCE:

150g butter

150g flour

1 litre milk, warmed

Good pinch of saffron

Method

For the pipérade:

Place all the ingredients in a saucepan and cook down slowly until all the liquid is cooked out of the onions and peppers.

For the bechamel sauce:

Melt the butter in a large pan and gradually stir in the flour. Cook for a few minutes without colouring.

Remove from the heat and allow to cool slightly then add the saffron.

Stir in the warmed milk gradually, bringing to the boil each time.

Place the fish in the sauce and then cook for a further 5 minutes.

To assemble:

Place a tablespoon of the pipérade in the bottom of an ovenproof dish, then spoon in the fish mixture. Top with the mashed potato and the grated parmesan. Bake at 180ºc for 20 minutes until piping hot and browned.

Goat's cheese deep dish tart with mixed bean cassoulet

Ingredients

FOR THE PASTRY:

250g plain flour

125g butter, cubed

1 teaspoon salt

1 egg yolks

1-2 tablespoons water to bind

FOR THE TART FILLING:

Half pint milk

Half pint cream

5 egg yolks

150g goat's cheese

Small bunch of tarragon leaves, chopped

1 teaspoon salt

FOR THE MIXED BEAN CASSOULET:

1 tin of cooked mixed beans (we soak dried beans overnight and then cook them, but for convenience a tin of cooked beans is quite acceptable)

100ml white wine

1 small onion, finely diced

1 clove garlic, crushed to a fine purée

100ml double cream

Juice of half a lemon

Salt

Tarragon, finely chopped

Method

For the pastry:

Sieve the flour into a bowl and rub in the butter rub until the mixture resembles breadcrumbs.

Add the salt, egg yolk and a tablespoon of the water and mix together to a smooth dough. Use extra water if necessary. Allow to rest in the fridge for 45 minutes. Roll out into a large sheet about the thickness of a pound coin and line an 22cm tart case.

Place a circular sheet of parchment in the bottom of the tart case and then line with baking beans. Bake at 170ºc for 20-30 minutes. Remove the baking beans and bake the tart case for a further 5 minutes.

To make the filling:

Whisk the egg yolks and pour on the cream and milk. Break in the goat's cheese and warm the mixture to around 30ºc over a bain marie. Add the chopped tarragon and salt.

Pour the filling into the tart case and bake at 130ºc for 45 minutes to an hour. The tart should still have a slight custardy wobble.

For the mixed bean cassoulet:

Sweat the onions and garlic in a small amount of oil until cooked and translucent. Add the mixed beans and wine and reduce by two-thirds. Stir in the cream and reduce by half. Season the beans with lemon juice and salt. Finish with the chopped tarragon.

Rolled ham hock with seeds and deep fried duck egg

Ingredients

FOR THE HAM HOCK:

2 ham hocks

50g sunflower seeds, pumpkin seeds and sesame seeds

4 carrots

4 sticks celery

1 onion, peeled and quartered

FOR THE DUCK EGG:

4 duck eggs

1 egg, beaten

Flour for dusting

50g breadcrumbs

Method

To cook the ham hock:

Cover the ham hock with cold water in a saucepan and add 2 of the carrots (roughly chopped) with 2 sticks of celery (roughly chopped) and the diced onion.

Bring to the boil and then turn down to a gentle simmer. Skim any white scum from the top of the pan and simmer for a further 3 hours or until the meat is falling from the bone.

Remove the ham hocks and allow to cool, reserve the ham stock for another recipe.

When cool enough to handle, remove the hock meat and discard the bones and skin.

Chop 2 carrots into ½cm cubes and sweat down in a small amount of vegetable oil until soft but not coloured.

Mix through the ham hock meat and the seeds and, whilst still warm, roll up in cling film into a fat sausage about 2 inches thick.

Leave to set in the fridge then slice into 4 even portions.

For the duck egg:

Place the duck eggs in a pan of boiling water and then boil for 6-7 minutes; place into iced water to stop the cooking process.

Peel the eggs and then roll in the flour, roll in the beaten egg then through the breadcrumbs.

Deep fry at 180ºc until golden.

To assemble:

Pan-fry the ham hocks on either side and then place in the oven to heat through at 180ºc for 8 minutes.

Mackerel cooked in a bag with aromatics

Ingredients

4 whole mackerel,
gutted and cleaned

150g chorizo

1 pak choi

1 lemon

1 lime

1 teaspoon pink peppercorns

1 teaspoon coriander seeds

4 star anise

4 cardamom pods

100g butter

200ml white wine

1 teaspoon salt

You'll also need some parchment
paper

Chef's Secret

Score the mackerel flesh with a sharp knife. This will allow the aromatics to penetrate the fish.

Method

Lay each fish in the middle of large sheets of parchment paper.

Place all the remaining ingredients except the wine inside and around the fish. Fold the paper over it once, so that you have a rectangular shape with 3 open sides. Fold each of the edges in turn several times over (the effect is rather like a concertina) to seal them and keep everything enclosed in the parcel. Before folding the last of the open edges, pour in the wine and then tuck the parchment under the fish.

Bake at 180°c for 15-20 minutes.

The Milestone ploughman's

This is a ploughman's with a difference – one where you make everything except the cheese (though don't let us stop you if the urge takes you!) It's a variation on the traditional hot water crust pastry pork pie. Fabulous served with our pickled balsamic onions.

Ingredients

FOR THE PASTRY:

1.5lb plain flour

4oz lard

Half a pint hot water

Pinch salt

Beaten egg for brushing

TO COOK THE HAM HOCKS:

2lb pork hocks

2 carrots

Half a head of celery

1 onion, peeled and diced

2 bay leaves

FOR THE PIE FILLING:

100g celery, diced

100g carrots

100g onion, finely diced

100g leeks, finely diced

30g flat leaf parsley, finely chopped

FOR THE PICKLED BALSAMIC ONIONS:

100g button onions, peeled

300ml balsamic vinegar

100g caster sugar

Method

For the pastry:

Bring the water to the boil and add the lard and allow to dissolve.

Using a food processor, blend together all the remaining ingredients and mix to a dough.

For the ham hocks:

Place the first 5 ingredients in a large pan and cover with cold water.

Bring to the boil. Skim off any scum and fat that rises to the top of the pan. Simmer the hocks for 3 hours until tender.

Remove the hocks from the cooking liquor. Flake off all the meat when they are cool enough to handle and discard the vegetables.

Pass the cooking liquor through a sieve and then reduce by half.

For the pie filling:

Sweat the vegetables in a teaspoon of oil until cooked but without colour and then mix with the hock meat and the parsley.

To assemble:

Roll out the pastry to the thickness of a pound coin and place in a terrine mould.

Add the filling and then place another layer of pastry on top to seal.

Bake at 160ºc for 1 hour 30 minutes then place on a rack and allow to cool.

Once properly cool, make a small hole in the top of the pastry and pour in the cooking liquour. Allow it to set in the fridge and then slice.

To make the pickled balsamic onions:

Place the onions, vinegar and sugar in a pan and cook for 20 minutes until the onions are softened and the balsamic vinegar has thickened slightly.

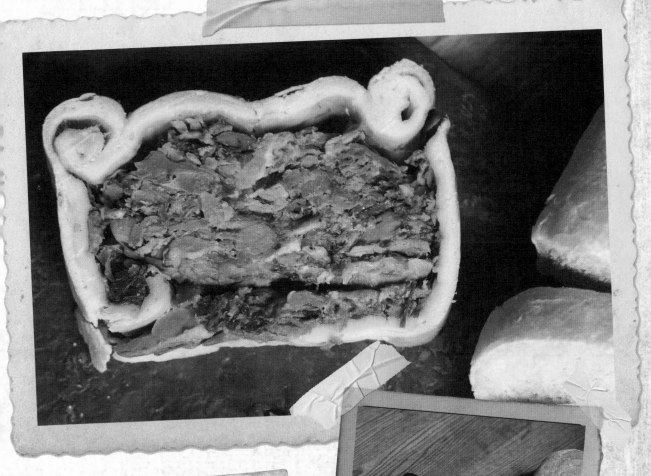

Chef's Secret
Don't be afraid of putting too much cooking liquor in your pie, it really makes it extra special.

Mussels, leeks, cider, bacon and clotted cream

Ingredients

2kg mussels, cleaned and washed

200g streaky bacon, cut into thin strips

4 cloves garlic, crushed to a purée

2 leeks

100g clotted cream

Half pint apple cider

Handful parsley, finely chopped

Method

Finely shred the leeks and then sweat down in a little oil in a deep pan with the garlic and bacon then cook until soft.

Turn up the heat and add the mussels.

Place a lid on top of the pan and steam for 2-3 minutes until the mussels open.

Add the clotted cream last and stir through.

Finish with the chopped parsley.

Chef's Secret

This is a West Country take on the classic French dish, moules marinière - try your own version with a local beer

Nettle gnocchi, globe artichoke, roast garlic purée, cep cream and braised baby gem lettuce

Ingredients

FOR THE NETTLE GNOCCHI:

600g floury potatoes, such as King Edwards or Estima, peeled

150g nettle leaves

2 free-range egg yolks

120g plain flour

FOR THE ARTICHOKES:

4 artichokes

Half bottle of white wine

Few sprigs of thyme

400ml water

1 teaspoon salt

100ml olive oil

2 lemons

Handful of parsley stalks

ROAST GARLIC PURÉE:

4 heads of garlic

50g butter

CEP CREAM:

125ml white wine

125ml vegetable stock

125ml double cream

10g dried ceps

Juice 1 lemon

Method

For the nettle gnocchi:

Roast the potatoes in their skins until soft. Scoop out the flesh and discard the skins. Mash the potatoes or pass through a sieve.

Blanch the nettle leaves for 20 seconds in boiling salted water and then refresh in iced water. Drain and then squeeze out any excess moisture. Chop finely or place in a food processor.

Sieve the flour into the potatoes and then add the yolks and nettle mix together. Roll out into inch wide sausages, cut out at half inch intervals.

Blanch in boiling water until the gnocchi floats, then refresh in iced water. Once cold, remove from the water.

For the artichokes:

To prepare the artichokes, first cut off the stalks from the base. Carefully snap or pull off enough layers of the tough, green outer leaves until you reach the ones that are mostly yellow and therefore more tender. Cut the tips off these, then peel the tough green outside of the base of the artichoke, using a potato peeler or sharp knife, until you see yellow. With a teaspoon, scrape out all the furry material inside the artichoke. Place all the ingredients in a pan and bring to the boil. Simmer for 2 minutes and then allow the artichokes to cool in the liquor.

Roast the garlic in the skins at 140ºc for 45 minutes. Squeeze the garlic from the skins and the blend to a smooth purée with the butter in a liquidiser. Pass through a fine sieve to ensure it is completely smooth.

For the cep cream:

Place the ceps and white wine in a pan and then reduce by half. Add the vegetable stock and then reduce by half again. Add the double cream and then reduce again by half. Season with salt and the lemon juice.

To assemble:

Shred 2 baby gem lettuces. Pan-fry the gnocchi and the artichokes to colour slightly. Add the lettuce and a splash of the cream. Allow the lettuce to wilt down. Place the cep cream in the bottom of a bowl and then add the gnocchi and artichoke mix on top.

Spread a small spoonful of the garlic purée on the side of the plate and serve.

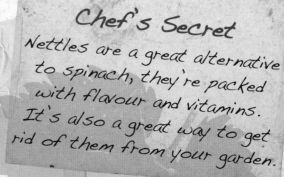

Chef's Secret

Nettles are a great alternative to spinach, they're packed with flavour and vitamins. It's also a great way to get rid of them from your garden.

Beef Bourguignon – slow cooked ox cheek, herb mashed potato and Bourguignon jus

Ingredients

4 ox cheeks

2 carrots, chopped

3 sticks celery, chopped

4 cloves garlic, crushed

Half bottle red wine

1 onion, peeled and quartered

(1 quantity of mash from the belly pork and black pudding dish on page 86)

1 handful of chopped parsley to add to the mash

FOR THE BOURGUIGNON

100g home cured bacon or pancetta, cut into 1 cm cubes

100g silverskin onions, peeled

Handful parsley, chopped

Ox cheek stock

1 large glass red wine

Method

To make the ox cheek:

Trim the fat from the ox cheek.

Heat the oil in a heavy-based frying pan and colour the ox cheeks on each side.

Remove and place in an ovenproof dish.

Colour the vegetables in the same pan and deglaze with the wine.

Reduce by two thirds and pour over the cheeks.

Cover with cold water and braise at 120ºc for 8 hours.

Once tender, remove the cheeks.

Strain and reduce the stock.

For the Bourguignon sauce:

Colour the bacon in a saucepan.

Add the onions and wine and reduce.

Combine with the stock and simmer for 30 minutes.

Place a scoop of the mashed potato in a bowl and top with the braised beef cheek then pour over the Bourguignon sauce.

Chef's Secret

Beef cheeks need plenty of slow cooking but they are probably the most flavoursome cut of beef if treated with respect.

Boned and rolled pig's head with mashed potato and caper jus

Ingredients

FOR THE PIG'S HEAD:

1 pig's head (this is more than enough so use the extra for another dish)

2 carrots, peeled and chopped

4 sticks celery, peeled and chopped

1 star anise

1 onion, peeled and chopped

1 leek, (white only)

Half bottle of white wine

2 cloves garlic

Water to cover

TO SERVE:

12 cherry tomatoes, roasted

16 caperberries

Mashed potato (page 86)

Reduced veal stock (page 158)

Method

For the pig's head:

To bone out the pig's head, run a boning knife from the top of the skull following the bone round one side. Be careful to keep the knife scraping the bone so you don't break the skin. Ensure all the flesh is removed from the cheeks. Repeat on the other side of the head.

Remove the ears from the head and then remove any hairs either with a razor or blowtorch.

Butterfly the cheek meat and then place half a tongue in each half of head.

Season with salt and then roll up into a sausage shape with the skin on the outside protecting all the meat.

Roll up tightly in cling film to hold the shape. Place the remaining ingredients in an ovenproof dish and then cover with water. Braise at 140ºc for 4-5 hours until tender. Take the pig's head out of the cooking liquor and allow to cool slightly.

When cool enough to handle, remove the cling film and then roll again tightly in more cling film to a neat cylinder. Use enough cling film to make it watertight and then place in iced water to cool.

To assemble:

Slice the pigs head into 4 portions and then pan-fry on each side to crisp up. Place in the oven at 170ºc until hot.

Sit on top of the mashed potato and top with the tomato, caperberries and reduced veal stock.

Chef's Secret

You may find pig's head difficult to obtain in the supermarket – if you ask your butcher in advance it won't be a problem to get hold of.

Salt mackerel and sesame seed pasty with tomato marmalade and sautéed new potatoes

Ingredients

FOR THE SALT MACKEREL:

600g mackerel fillets, skin off and pinboned

250g Maldon sea salt

125g caster sugar

FOR THE FILLING:

50g each of leek, carrots, onions and celery, all peeled and diced into small cubes

1 tablespoon sesame oil

FOR THE PASTRY:

500g plain flour

250g unsalted butter

1 egg yolk

1 tablespoon water to bind

1 teaspoon salt

FOR THE TOMATO MARMALADE:

2 tins chopped tomatoes

100ml white wine vinegar

1 red chilli, finely chopped and seeds discarded

1 teaspoon paprika

100g caster sugar

Half onion, finely chopped

Method

For the filling:

Mix the salt and sugar together and then rub all over the mackerel fillets. Place on a tray and cover with cling film, then put in the fridge for three hours.

Wash the fillets in cold water and pat dry with kitchen roll. Cut into 2cm cubes.

Meanwhile, sweat the vegetables in a saucepan with the sesame oil until soft but without colouring. Allow to cool and then mix with the mackerel.

To make the pastry:

Mix the flour, salt and butter together until it resembles fine breadcrumbs.

Add the egg yolk and water. Mix together into a smooth dough. Be careful not to overwork the mix.

Wrap in cling film and allow to rest in the fridge for 1 hour.

To assemble the pasties:

Roll out the pastry to the thickness of a pound coin and then cut out an oval shape. Place some of the mackerel filling in the middle of the pastry then fold into the middle, sealing the pasty with a light layer of egg yolk. Crimp the pastry at the seam and then brush with beaten egg. Sprinkle with sesame seeds and allow to rest in the fridge for 30 minutes.

Bake at 180°c for 15-20 minutes.

To make the tomato marmalade:

Place the onion in a saucepan with a teaspoon of oil and sweat until soft but not coloured. Add the remaining ingredients then cook down till reduced by half (the marmalade should have a nice gloss and a sweet and sour taste).

To assemble:

Boil some new potatoes in salted water then pan-fry them in a little oil until golden. Mix with two tablespoons of the tomato marmalade. Finally, place a handful of spinach over the hot dish and allow it to wilt.

Stuffed pig's trotters

Ingredients

4 pigs trotters (ask your butcher for the large ones from the back legs)

200g pork mince

600g ham hock, cooked in the same way as for the ham and eggs on page 96

10g sage

1 egg yolk

FOR THE COOKING LIQUOR:

3 carrots

2 sticks of celery

1 bulb of garlic, chopped in half

1 onion, peeled and quartered

4 pints water

TO FINISH:

50g butter

50g honey

Method

For the liquor:

Place all the ingredients for the cooking liquor in a pan and bring to the boil. Turn down the heat and simmer for 30 minutes.

Prepare the trotters:

Bone the trotters out by using a sharp knife to cut just under the skin, running along the bone and peeling the skin back. Work carefully to ensure the skin is not punctured.

Remove the bone by cutting through at the knuckle. You will be left with what resembles a sock of skin.

Finely chop the sage and mix the with the pork mince, hock and egg yolk. Season with salt. Stuff the trotter skin, wrap in cling film to hold the shape and poach for 45 minutes in the cooking liquor.

Remove the trotters from the pan and place into a non-stick frying pan with the butter and honey and glaze before serving.

Serve with seasonal greens and roasted root vegetables.

Pan-fried plaice fillet with lemon pith purée, roast crayfish tails, muscat grapes, crayfish & elderflower velouté

Ingredients

1 fillet of plaice (about 6oz)

16 live crayfish

16 seedless white grapes

2 lemons

1 bulb of fennel

2 sticks of celery

Half a leek, white only

1 star anise

50ml Noilly Prat

1 small glass white wine

10 elderflower heads or dried elderflower

1 teaspoon tomato purée

A few pea shoots

TO MAKE THE LEMON PITH PURÉE:

2 lemons

75g sugar

30g butter

Method

To make the shellfish bisque:

To dispatch the crayfish, plunge into boiling salted water. Boil for 3 minutes, then refresh in iced water to stop the cooking process.

Peel the tails from the crayfish as you would a prawn and then reserve the shells and head for the sauce.

Clean the shells and heads of the crayfish and then roast at 180ºc for 15 minutes.

Finely chop the fennel, celery and leek and sweat down with a small amount of oil until softened.

Pour in the wine and Noilly Prat and reduce until there is barely any liquid left.

Add the tomato purée and cook for 2 minutes on a low heat.

Cover the crayfish shells with the water, star anise and lemon zest. Simmer for 30 minutes.

Add the elderflowers and place in a food processor. Blend until a fine sauce.

Pass the sauce through a fine strainer then reduce until thickened.

Season with salt and a squeeze of lemon juice.

To make the lemon pith purée:

Zest the lemons and set aside for the bisque. Squeeze them and save the juice.

Place the pith in a pan and cover with water. Bring to the boil and then refresh in cold water. Repeat twice more (this helps remove the bitterness from the pith).

Place the pith, sugar and butter in a liquidiser and blend to a fine purée. Pass through a fine sieve and season with salt.

To assemble:

Pan-fry the plaice in a non-stick pan until golden. Pour the lemon juice into the pan along with the butter, then the cooked crayfish and the grapes to heat through and glaze the plaice with the butter.

Spread the pith purée on a plate followed by the plaice, grapes and crayfish. Finish with the bisque and pea shoots.

Chef's Secret

The freshwater Signal crayfish are a pest and are killing our native crayfish. Do your part for the environment and eat more of them!

Poussin, chateau potatoes, chicken velouté, sage crisps

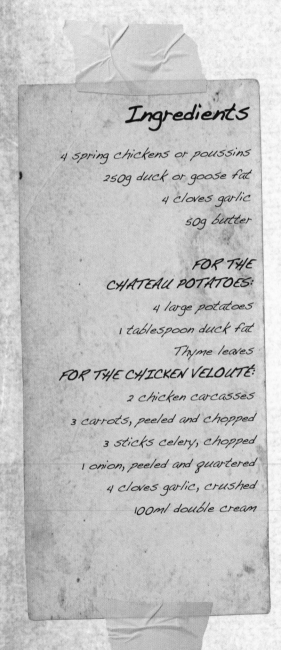

Ingredients

4 spring chickens or poussins

250g duck or goose fat

4 cloves garlic

50g butter

FOR THE CHATEAU POTATOES:

4 large potatoes

1 tablespoon duck fat

Thyme leaves

FOR THE CHICKEN VELOUTÉ:

2 chicken carcasses

3 carrots, peeled and chopped

3 sticks celery, chopped

1 onion, peeled and quartered

4 cloves garlic, crushed

100ml double cream

Method

To prepare the chicken:

Remove the legs from the carcass and then trim through to free the crown.

Place the legs in a ovenproof dish. Coat with the duck fat, cover with tin foil and then place in a pre-heated oven at 120ºc for 1 hour 30 minutes until tender.

Remove the legs from the confit fat and allow to cool.

To roast the crown, place in a frying pan skin side down until golden and crisp. Turn over and colour. Add a few sprigs of thyme, a clove of garlic and the butter to the pan. Top up with water until the chicken is half submerged. Place in the oven at 180ºc for 10 minutes.

For the chateau potatoes:

Peel the potatoes with a paring knife and turn into barrel shapes. Place the duck fat in a pan and colour the potatoes. Transfer to a roasting tin, sprinkle on the thyme leaves and roast at 170ºc for 35 minutes until soft and golden.

Chicken velouté:

Place all the ingredients except the cream into a pan and cover with cold water. Bring to the boil and then turn down to a simmer. Skim off the white scum and cook out for 1 hour 30 minutes on a gentle simmer.

Pass the stock through a fine strainer and then skim any remaining fat or scum away.

Add the cream and reduce until a glossy sauce consistency.

To assemble:

Place the legs skin side down in a hot pan until crisp, then top with the chicken crown.

Place the chateau potatoes on the plate and then finish with the sauce. Add a few deep fried sage leaves for a garnish if the mood takes you.

Chef's Secret

Here's a great way of cooking chicken. The water in the pan will keep the chicken moist whilst still crisping the skin.

Rabbit loin, carrot purée, sauted lettuce with rabbit leg, courgette and pigs tail cannelloni and a rabbit jus

Ingredients

2 wild rabbits

4 pig's tails

2 carrots, chopped

2 sticks celery, chopped

1 onion, peeled and quartered

Few sprigs thyme

Few sprigs rosemary

FOR THE CANNELLONI:

Braised rabbit meat and pig's tail

Handful parsley, finely chopped

2 courgettes, thinly sliced

2 teaspoons rabbit stock, reduced

FOR THE CARROT PURÉE:

2 carrots, peeled and finely chopped

20ml honey

30g butter

FOR THE BRAISED BABY GEM LETTUCE:

50g butter

100ml chicken stock

2 baby gem lettuce

Method

To prepare the rabbit:

Remove the legs from the rabbit and set aside for braising.

Cut off the loin and set aside.

Place the carrots, onion and celery, rabbit legs, pig's tail and rabbit carcass into an ovenproof dish and cover with cold water.

Create a tin foil lid and cook in a pre-heated oven at 140ºc for 2 hours.

Remove the meat from the liquid and allow to cool.

Cut the meat off the pig's tail and rabbit legs, discarding any bones.

Strain the cooking liquid, skim off excess fat and reduce.

To make the cannelloni:

Blanch the courgette strips in boiling water for 5 seconds.

Refresh in iced water.

Remove from the water and pat dry.

Mix the remaining ingredients together and roll into a thin cylinder.

Overlap the courgette strips on a sheet of cling film.

Lay the meat on the courgette and roll into a cannelloni.

Tie each end of the cling film, ensuring it is watertight.

For the carrot purée:

Place carrots and honey in a saucepan and cover with water.

Bring to the boil and cook until soft.

Liquidise with a tablespoon of cooking liquid and blend into a fine purée.

Add the butter and mix to emulsify.

Pass through a fine sieve and season with salt.

For the baby gem lettuce:

Rub the lettuce with butter and set in the fridge.

Place into a hot frying pan to colour.

Add the stock and remaining butter and cook over a high heat.

Baste with butter and stock and season with a pinch of salt.

To assemble:

Pan-fry the rabbit loins.

Place the cannelloni in boiling water and heat through.

Spread a spoonful of purée on a plate.

Top with the cannelloni, rabbit loin and lettuce.

Drizzle the rabbit stock over the dish.

Rack of lamb, wild garlic purée, wilted spinach with a trompette jus

Ingredients

4 x four bone best end of lamb, French trimmed

TO MAKE THE VEAL STOCK/TROMPETTE JUS:

4kg veal bones

2 calves feet

4 litres water

400g carrots, chopped

200g onions, chopped

100g celery, chopped

1kg tomatoes

200g trompette mushrooms

Bouquet garni

4 cloves garlic

200g spinach, wilted

FOR THE PURÉE:

300g wild garlic leaves

Method

For the wild garlic purée:

Bring a large pan of water to the boil. Blanch the wild garlic for 10 seconds then transfer to a liquidiser. Blend with a small amount of the blanching water until a fine smooth purée.

For the stock:

In a very large pan, brown the bones and feet in a little oil. Place the bones in a stock pot, cover with cold water and bring to simmer.

Roast the onions, carrots and celery with fat from bones. Drain off fat and add vegetables to stock and deglaze the tray. Add tomatoes, mushrooms and garlic and simmer for 10 hours. Skim frequently.

Strain and reduce until the sauce thickens and has an intense flavour. Finally, add the trompette mushrooms.

For the lamb rack:

Heat oil in a large frying pan. Cook the lamb to colour all over then turn so that the fatty skin side is downwards. Cook for a few minutes, then place the lamb in the oven at 180ºc for 8-16 minutes depending on how pink you want your lamb. Wilt a few spinach leaves in a pan with a small amount of butter and season with salt.

To assemble:

Spread a line of the purée on a plate. Spoon on the spinach. Cut the lamb rack in half, place on the plate and pour over a small amount of the jus and trompette mushrooms.

Chef's Secret

Wild garlic grows in wooded conditions next to waterways from March to May.

You'll smell the heavy garlic aroma before you spot the plant.

Don't pick wild plants to eat unless you're an experienced forager.

Rump beef and chestnuts, braised short ribs, tea-infused fondant potato with beef jus

Ingredients

4 x 6oz rump steaks, trimmed of any sinew and fat

4 x 6oz short rib pieces

4 large potatoes

3 Earl Grey teabags

200ml beef stock

50g butter

2 carrots

2 celery sticks

1 onion, peeled and quartered

Few sprigs thyme and rosemary

Half bottle red wine

100g pre-cooked chestnuts

Method

For the potatoes:

Using a ring cutter, cut out cylinders of potato, trim off any skin and neaten the shape. Pan-fry each of the fondants in a little vegetable oil on each side until golden. Add the stock, butter and tea bags and then place in a pre-heated oven at 170°c for 45 minutes until soft.

For the braised shortribs:

Pan-fry the ribs on each side to get a good colour. Remove from the pan and replace with the onion, celery and carrot. Cook until brown. Remove from the pan and place in an ovenproof container with the ribs. Add the wine to the pan. Deglaze and then reduce by two-thirds. Pour over the ribs, add the thyme and rosemary and top up with cold water. Cover with foil and cook at 150°c for 4 hours until tender.

Remove from the cooking liquor and strain, skim off any fat and reduce down to an intensely-flavoured sauce.

To assemble:

Pan-fry the rump steaks until rare and allow to rest. Cook the chestnuts in the same pan as the meat and then arrange the rump, shortrib, fondant potato and chestnuts on a plate. Finish with the sauce.

Chef's Secret

This is a great way to serve beef, one piece rare, one piece slow cooked and meltingly tender. Two great textures on one plate.

Rump beef, sweetbread, oxtail and tongue cottage pie watercress purée

Ingredients

4 x 170g beef rump portions, trimmed

100ml veal jus, reduced

1 ox tongue

2 carrots

2 sticks celery

3 cloves garlic

1 onion, peeled and quartered

Thyme leaves

See Watercress purée on page 134

To cook the oxtail – see turbot poached in merlot recipe on page 130

FOR THE COTTAGE PIE:

1 carrot, peeled and chopped into half centimetre cubes

1 stick celery, peeled and chopped into half centimetre cubes

50g peas

200g mashed potato

FOR THE SWEETBREADS:

200g sweetbreads

2 carrots

2 sticks celery

3 cloves garlic

1 onion, peeled and quartered

500ml water

Method

To make the cottage pie filling:

Place the ox tongue in a saucepan, cover with water and bring to the boil.

Run cold water onto the pan to refresh.

Cover in cold water and add the remaining ingredients.

Bring to the boil and simmer for 2 hours and 30 minutes.

When cool, peel the skin off the tongue and dice into 1cm cubes.

Mix the tongue, tail, sweetbreads, vegetables and oxtail cooking juices in a saucepan and cook until tender.

Place the mix into individual cottage pie dishes and top with the mashed potato.

Cook at 180°c for 15 minutes or until glazed.

To make the sweetbreads:

Place the ingredients in a saucepan and bring to the boil.

Simmer for 10 minutes.

Add the sweetbreads and poach for 15 minutes.

Remove the liquid and cool in iced water.

Peel the outer membrane from the sweetbreads and slice into 1cm cubes.

To assemble:

Pan-fry the steak with a little butter and thyme leaves until rare.

Warm the watercress purée and spread onto a plate.

Add the steak and cottage pie.

Drizzle over the veal stock.

Chef's Secret

Cottage pie with a Milestone twist, using offal rather than traditional minced meat.

Pan-fried salmon with roasted radish, nettle gnocchi, crab faggots and lemon balm emulsion

Ingredients

4 x 170g salmon portions

FOR THE CRAB FAGGOT:

120g brown crab meat

120g white crab meat

4 iceberg lettuce leaves

1 red chilli, de-seeded and finely chopped

Small handful fresh coriander

1 shallot, finely diced

1 tablespoon crème fraîche

1 lime, juiced and zested

FOR THE LEMON BALM EMULSION:

Large handful lemon balm, finely chopped

1 egg yolk

100ml vegetable oil

20ml water

10ml white wine vinegar

Half teaspoon lethicin powder

12 breakfast radishes

Nettle gnocchi see the recipe on page 104

Method

Lemon balm emulsion:

Whisk the white wine vinegar, egg yolk and lethecin until light, pale and doubled in size.

Slowly pour in the oil and whisk constantly.

Add the water slowly whilst whisking.

Season with salt and add finely chopped lemon balm.

To make the crab faggot:

Mix the crab meat, crème fraîche, lime juice and zest, shallot, chilli and coriander.

Season with salt and place in refrigerator until ready to use.

Remove the tough stalk from the middle of the lettuce and blanch the leaves in boiling salted water for 8 seconds until wilted.

Squeeze excess water from the leaves.

Place a ball of the crab mix in the centre of each leaf.

Roll into a tight ball and wrap in cling film, ensuring it is watertight.

For the nettle gnocchi:

See recipe on page 104.

To assemble:

Pan-fry the salmon, skin side down, until crisp and golden.

Turn on each side to seal.

Place in the oven at 180ºc for 5 minutes.

Cut the radish in half and pan-fry with the gnocchi.

Place the crab in a pan of boiling water to heat.

Dress the plate with the lemon balm emulsion.

Lay the radish and gnocchi on top and place the crab faggot to one side.

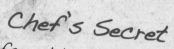

127

Salmon with a cardamom crust, sautéed new potatoes, cucumber and caper dressing

Ingredients

4 x 6oz salmon portions, skinless

300g boiled new potatoes, cooked and cooled

1 cucumber, halved and de-seeded

CAPER DRESSING:

30g capers drained from their brine

1 small bunch parsley, chopped

50ml olive oil

20ml white wine vinegar

CARDAMOM CRUST:

3 cardamoms pods, crushed

1 large handful parsley, finely chopped

1 large handful of coriander, finely chopped

50g breadcrumbs

1 egg yolk

Method

Caper dressing:

Fry the capers with a teaspoon of oil in a non-stick frying pan until they are nice and crisp. Remove from the pan and place in a mixing bowl with the vinegar and oil. Whisk to emulsify. Add the finely chopped parsley and season to taste with salt

For the cardamom crust:

In a dry frying pan toast the cardamom pods to release the essential oils and then crush to a paste in a pestle and mortar. Place the remaining ingredients in a food processor, including the cardamom and pulse to reduce to a fine paste. Place a layer of the crust about the thickness of a pound coin on top of the salmon and then allow to rest in the fridge for 30 minutes.

To finish:

Place the salmon in the oven at 180ºc for 10-12 minutes. Heat a non-stick pan with a splash of vegetable oil and saute the new potatoes and cucumber. Place the cucumber and potatoes in the centre of the dish. Rest the salmon on top and dress the dish with the caper dressing.

Turbot poached in red wine with oxtail, spinach and baby onions

Ingredients

200g spinach, wilted

FOR THE OXTAIL:

1kg oxtail

2 carrots

2 sticks celery

1 onion, peeled and quartered

4 cloves garlic

Few sprigs thyme

Few sprigs rosemary

Half bottle red wine

Water to cover

FOR THE TURBOT:

4 x 170g turbot portions, skin left on

Half bottle merlot or other full bodied red wine

FOR THE RED WINE ONIONS:

6 button onions

250ml red wine

50g caster sugar

Method

To make the turbot:

Bring the red wine to the boil in a saucepan and add the turbot.

Reduce to a simmer until cooked. The fish will flake easily if cooked.

To make the oxtail:

Pan-fry the oxtail until golden and place in an ovenproof dish.

In the frying pan, cook the vegetables until coloured.

Add the red wine and reduce by two thirds.

Add the vegetables and red wine to the ovenproof dish and cover with water.

Create a tin foil lid and cook in the oven at 140ºc for 5 hours until tender.

Remove the oxtail and allow to cool.

Strip the meat from the bones, discarding all bones.

Transfer the cooking liquid to a sauce pan and reduce to a thick sauce consistency.

To make the sauce:

Peel the onions, leaving the roots intact to prevent it breaking apart.

Place the red wine, sugar and onions in a saucepan and simmer for 1 hour until soft.

To assemble:

Place the spinach in the bottom of a bowl.

Lay the turbot and oxtail on top of the spinach.

Scatter pieces of onion on each plate and drizzle with the sauce.

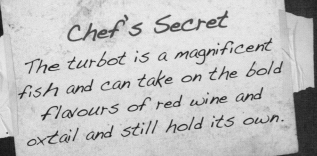

Venison heart meatballs in a tomato sauce with watercress pilaf rice

Ingredients

FOR THE MEATBALLS:

500g venison heart mince

300g venison mince

1 teaspoon piri piri flakes

1 egg yolk to bind

Flour to dust with

Salt

FOR THE TOMATO SAUCE:

1 onion finely diced

1 teaspoon piri piri flakes

2 cloves garlic

175ml red wine

4 tins chopped tomatoes

1 teaspoon thyme leaves

20ml balsamic vinegar

20g caster sugar

FOR THE RICE PILAF:

220g long grain rice

500ml vegetable stock

FOR THE WATERCRESS PURÉE:

200g watercress washed

Method

For the meatballs:

Mix all the ingredients together except the flour and then cook a small piece of the meatball mix. Taste the seasoning and adjust if required.

Roll into balls and coat with flour and then colour in a frying pan with a little oil.

Place in a roasting tray and then bake at 180ºc for 20-30 minutes, depending on the size of the meatballs, check to see they are cooked through.

For the tomato sauce:

Finely dice the onion and garlic and then cook with the chilli flakes until soft but with no colour.

Add the red wine and reduce by two thirds.

Add the remaining ingredients and reduce further by a quarter.

Blend the sauce in a liquidiser and then pass through a sieve.

Add the meatballs and leave to marinate in the sauce, preferably overnight but an hour will suffice.

For the rice:

Place the rice and stock into an ovenproof dish and cover with cling film.

Cook at 170ºc for 20-30 minutes until the rice is soft.

For the watercress purée:

Bring a large pan of water to the boil and then add the watercress for 10 seconds until wilted, remove and then purée in a liquidiser with a small amount of the cooking liquor until smooth.

To assemble:

Warm the meatballs in the sauce. Warm the rice with a teaspoon of water and add the watercress purée.

Place the rice on the bottom of the plate and top with the meatballs and sauce. Garnish with watercress.

Chef's Secret

You may find venison hearts difficult to obtain, why not substitute for lambs heart. This is a real thrifty dish but packed with flavour.

Sous vide venison loin, nettle and haunch wellington, watercress purée, beetroot fondant, braised baby gem lettuce and game gravy

Ingredients

FOR THE VENISON HAUNCH:

450g venison haunch
2 large carrots, chopped
1 large white onion, peeled and chopped
1 leek, chopped
2 garlic cloves, crushed
2 celery sticks, chopped
Small bunch thyme
100ml port
250ml merlot
150ml chicken stock
500ml venison stock

FOR THE PANCAKES:

100g plain flour
1 egg
1 egg yolk
Pinch salt
285ml milk
200g nettles, wilted and puréed
10g butter, melted

FOR THE PUFF PASTRY:

200g plain flour, plus extra for dusting
Pinch salt
200g butter, at room temperature
125ml ice cold water
1 egg yolk, for brushing

FOR THE WELLINGTON:

1 egg yolk, beaten with 2 tablespoons water

FOR THE VENISON LOIN:

1 450g venison loin
20g butter
4 thyme sprigs, each wrapped in cling film
Sunflower oil
Sea salt and freshly ground black pepper

FOR THE GRAVY:

100g butter
750g mushrooms, finely sliced
350g shallots, finely sliced
350g venison trim, diced
100ml sherry vinegar
700ml red wine
500ml veal stock
1 litre venison stock

FOR THE WATERCRESS PURÉE:

250g watercress
50g spinach
25g flat leaf parsley, picked
10g butter

FOR THE BEETROOT FONDANT:

4 large beetroot
150ml chicken stock
25g butter
Few thyme sprigs

FOR THE BABY GEMS:

2 baby gem lettuce, cut in half and outer leaves trimmed
50g butter
150ml vegetable stock

Chef's Secret

This recipe, though very complex is well worth the effort as it helped us win the title of 'Best British' in Gordon Ramsay's Best Restaurant competition.

Sous vide venison loin method

For the venison haunch:

Preheat the oven to 120°c.

Trim the venison and cut into 2cm cubes.

Heat sunflower oil in a pan and fry the cubes to form a rich brown seal.

Remove the meat and add the carrot, onion, leek, garlic and celery.

Add the thyme to infuse the oil.

Remove the vegetables and pour in the port and wine to deglaze the pan.

Reduce by half and pour into an ovenproof dish with the remaining ingredients.

Cover with foil and braise in the oven for 8 hours.

Remove from oven and allow to cool then shred the meat with a fork.

Pass the braising liquid through a sieve and reduce to 100ml.

Mix the stock into the shredded meat and roll in cling film into a cylinder.

Allow to set in the refrigerator for 1-1 hour 30 minutes.

For the pancakes:

Whisk together the flour and add the egg yolk, milk and nettles. Fold in the butter.

Leave to rest for at least 30 minutes.

Heat the sunflower oil in a non-stick pan.

Pour the batter into the pan, to your desired thickness.

Cook on both sides until golden.

For the puff pastry:

Sift together the flour and the salt and rub in the butter. Stir in enough of the water to make a soft dough, wrap in cling film and chill for 20 minutes.

Put the butter between 2 pieces of greaseproof paper and flatten out with a rolling pin until it is a rectangle 10 x 7.5cm.

Roll out the dough to another rectangle that measures 12.5 x 25cm.

Take the butter out of the paper and put on the dough rectangle. Bring the corners of the dough together to make an envelope. Chill for 10 minutes.

Roll out the envelope on a floured surface to make a rectangle that is 3 times longer than it is wide. Fold one third into the middle and then the other third on top.

Seal the edges lightly with a rolling pin and turn the pastry 90 degrees. Repeat and chill for 30 minutes.

Repeat this rolling and folding twice more and then chill for another 30 minutes and then do 2 more – the pastry will have been rolled and folded 6 times altogether.

Now roll out and use as required.

It is important that the pastry is well chilled otherwise the pastry will become greasy and tough when baked. Also the butter might come through the surface, if this happens, dab on a little flour.

To make the wellington:

Preheat the oven to 180°c.

Roll the pastry to a 3mm thickness.

Cut into a square of 125mm x 125 mm.

Cut a pancake into a square of 125mm x 125mm.

Place the pancake atop the pastry.

Place the 80g of braised venison in the centre on top of the pancake.

Roll the edges together to make an individual portion.

Brush with the egg wash and sprinkle with sea salt.

Refrigerate for 15 minutes before baking for 15-20 minutes.

To make the venison loin:

Trim off any sinews from the venison loin.

Cut into 4 portions and place each in a vacuum pouch with 5g butter.

Place a cling film wrapped spring of thyme in each pouch and vacuum pack.

Place in a water bath set to 54°c for 20-25 minutes.

Once cooked, remove from the pouch and pat dry.

Heat a drizzle of sunflower oil in a pan and colour the venison.

For the gravy:

Heat the butter in the pan, caramelise the shallots and mushrooms and strain.

Heat the remaining butter in another pan and caramelise the venison until golden. Deglaze the pans with the vinegar.

In a separate pan, reduce the wine by half.

Add the stock and remaining ingredients. Reduce to a sauce consistency and strain.

To make the watercress purée:

Wash the cress, spinach and parsley and drain well.

Blanch in a deep pan of boiling water for 10 seconds and drain.

Blend with a stick blender into a purée.

Add the butter to emulsify and season with salt.

Pass through a fine sieve into a metal bowl. This will help to chill the purée and prevent colour loss.

To make the beetroot fondant:

Peel the beetroot.

Using a 38mm ring cutter, cut each beetroot.

Trim the beetroot discs to 25mm high and neaten the edges.

Place in a hot frying pan to colour.

Lay in a shallow dish with the chicken stock, butter and thyme and bake in the oven at 180°c for 20-30 minutes.

To make the baby gem lettuce:

Rub the lettuce with 20g butter and place in the refrigerator to set.

Colour the gem halves in a frying pan.

Add the stock and remaining butter and cook on a high heat, basting the lettuce.

Season with a pinch of salt.

To assemble:

Spread a small spoonful of the purée across the plate.

Place the loin, wellington and fondant alongside.

Rest the baby gem atop the fondant and spoon the gravy over the loin.

Chef's Secret

As you can see, puff pastry is a labour of love, good quality pre-made puff pastry is acceptable and easily available.

Yorkshire pudding, braised shin of beef and root vegetables

Ingredients

FOR THE SHIN OF BEEF:

1kg beef shin, cut into 4 pieces

100g flour

2 carrots, peeled and chopped

3 sticks celery, chopped

1 onion, peeled and quartered

Few sprigs thyme

Few sprigs rosemary

Half bottle red wine

5 cloves garlic

FOR THE YORKSHIRE PUDDING:

100g plain flour

3 eggs

200ml milk

Pinch of salt

5 ice cubes

ROOT VEGETABLES:

2 carrots

1 swede

4 parsnips

1 tablespoon honey

50g butter

Method

To make the beef shin:

In a heavy frying pan add the vegetable oil and gently fry to colour the beef.

Remove the beef from the pan and add the vegetables, fry these until slightly coloured also.

Add the red wine and reduce by two thirds.

Place all the ingredients in an ovenproof dish and cover with water.

Create a tin foil lid and braise at 140ºc for 5 hours until tender.

Remove the meat from the liquid, strain the stock through a fine sieve and reduce, this will be used for the sauce.

For the Yorkshire pudding:

Mix together all the ingredients except the ice cubes.

Place the ice cubes in a fine sieve and pour the mixture through over the ice cubes.

Pour a small amount of oil in a large Yorkshire pudding tray in the oven at 200ºc until smoking.

Fill with the Yorkshire pudding mix and cook for 25-30 minutes.

To roast the root vegetables:

Peel all the vegetables and chop into 3cm cubes.

Melt the butter in a frying pan, add the vegetables and colour.

Add honey and roast at 180ºc for 20-25 minutes until soft.

To assemble:

Place the root vegetables inside the Yorkshire pudding.

Top with the beef shin and the reduced sauce.

Baked apple stuffed with raisins, custard with rum and raisin ice cream

Ingredients

FOR THE BAKED APPLES:

4 Braeburn apples, cored

50g fresh bread crumbs

75g demerara sugar

30g raisins

75ml dark rum

FOR THE CUSTARD:

250ml milk

250ml double cream

50g caster sugar

1 vanilla pod

6 large egg yolks

For the ice cream see our basic recipe on page 160

Method

For the baked apples:

Soak the raisins in the rum with half the sugar for 24 hours. Press a small ball of breadcrumbs into one end of the cored apples to seal the hole. Combine the rum and remaining sugar and stuff the apples until full to the brim. Pour in any of the rum that the raisins have not soaked up.

Wrap the apples in tin foil and bake at 170°c for 20-25 minutes until the apples are soft.

To make home-made custard:

Place the milk, vanilla and cream in a saucepan and bring to the boil. Whisk together the yolks and sugar until light and pale. Add the milk and cream mix and continue whisking. Simmer until the mixture thickens enough to coat the back of a wooden spoon. Do not allow to boil as this will make the custard scramble.

Bakewell tart with amaretto ice cream

Ingredients

FOR THE FRANGIPANE MIX:

160g diced unsalted butter, at room temperature

160g icing sugar

160g ground almonds

30g plain flour (sieved twice)

4 small or 3 large eggs (beaten)

FOR THE SWEET PASTRY:

1 lemon, zested

225g plain flour

75g sugar

150g diced well-chilled unsalted butter

3g salt (if using unsalted butter)

1 egg yolk

1 whole egg

150g raspberry jam

For the amaretto ice cream see our basic recipe on page 160

Method

Frangipane mix:

In a bowl, cream eggs and butter, adding one egg at a time to the butter. Once all eggs are incorporated add all remaining ingredients, stir to combine then chill.

Sweet pastry:

Place all dry ingredients in mixing bowl. Slowly incorporate butter using a rubbing-in method with the tips of your fingers until the mixture is a sandy consistency

Beat the eggs together and add, mix until a soft dough texture then refrigerate in the fridge for a minimum of 1 hour.

Roll pastry until thin. Place in tart cases then blind bake with baking beans on top of a layer of parchment for approximately 20 minutes on 180°c. Keep checking during baking. Remove from the oven. Leave in the cases to cool but remove the baking beans.

To assemble:

Spread a thin layer of raspberry jam onto the tart case

Fill the tart case two thirds full of your frangipane mixture and bake at 185°c until golden and firm.

Remove the tart from the case and leave to cool on a cooling rack.

Chilled peach and Champagne soup with strawberry pannacotta

Ingredients

FOR THE SOUP:

1kg slightly overripe peaches

200ml Champagne

300g caster sugar

Juice of half a lemon

FOR THE PANNACOTTA:

300ml double cream

300ml strawberry purée (made from 400g strawberries, 100g caster sugar, 50ml water cooked till soft then blended in a liquidiser and passed through a fine sieve)

50g caster sugar

4 sheets gelatine (soaked in cold water till soft)

Method

To make the soup:

Halve the peaches and stone them.

Place in an ovenproof dish and cover with tin foil then roast for 20 minutes at 180ºc.

Meanwhile place the Champagne and lemon juice in a saucepan with the sugar and heat until dissolved.

Put the peaches and the Champagne mixture in a liquidiser and blend until really smooth. Pass the mixture through a fine sieve, using a ladle to push the mix through.

Taste and if necessary add more sugar – the actual amount will depend on how ripe the peaches are.

Chill the soup in the fridge until ready to serve.

For the panncotta:

Place the cream, strawberry purée and caster sugar in a saucepan and bring to the boil.

Take the gelatine out of the water and squeeze out any excess liquid then whisk into the cream and strawberry mix.

Once fully dissolved place into dariole moulds (metal moulds) and allow to set in the fridge.

To assemble:

Dip the dariole moulds into boiling water for 2 seconds to help the pannacotta turn out.

Place in a bowl and then half fill with the peach soup.

Garnish with fresh strawberry quarters and serve.

Chocolate and beetroot cake with cinder toffee

Ingredients

FOR THE CAKE:

250g dark chocolate (melted)

3 eggs

1kg demerara sugar

2 tablespoons black treacle

2 tablespoons honey

40g self-raising flour

40g plain flour

Pinch of bicarbonate of soda

Pinch of salt

25g cocoa

50g ground almonds

250g raw finely grated beetroot

100ml beetroot juice reduction (reduced from 200ml)

30ml sunflower oil

BEETROOT HONEYCOMB:

75g honey

140g glucose

400g caster sugar

5 tablespoons beetroot juice reduction (reduced from 10 tablespoons)

20g bicarbonate of soda

Melted chocolate to coat

Method

For the cake:

Whisk the sugar, salt, honey, treacle and egg in an electric mixer until the ingredients double in size.

Fold in the flour, cocoa, almonds and bicarbonate.

Fold in the beetroot, chocolate, beetroot juice and oil.

Bake for 1 hour at 140ºc in a large cake ring.

For the cinder toffee:

Boil the honey, glucose, sugar and beetroot juice in a heavy-based saucepan till it reaches 150ºc on a sugar thermometer.

Sieve the bicarbonate twice and add to mix.

Stir through quickly then pour onto baking tray lined with a Silpat (a non-stick baking mat).

Once cooled, break into small pieces and dip into the chocolate.

Chef's Secret

This recipe may sound unusual but it really works as the sweetness of the beetroot balances the bitterness of the chocolate.

Chocolate and frangipane cake with figs, red wine ripple ice cream, red wine syrup and crushed hazelnuts

Serves 6

Ingredients

FOR THE CAKE:

250g ground almonds

150g hazelnuts, crushed

250g butter

250g icing sugar

3 eggs

2 egg yolks

50g plain flour

50g cocoa powder

For the ice cream see our basic recipe on page 160

FOR A RED WINE SYRUP:

500ml red wine

200g caster sugar

TO GARNISH:

12 figs cut in half

Handfull of hazelnuts, crushed

Method

To make the cake:

Cream the butter and sugar with an electric whisk until light and fluffy. Add the almonds, flour and cocoa and whisk in, followed by the eggs (one at a time) and whisk in. Add the crushed hazelnuts. Place in a baking tray lined with baking parchment and bake at 150ºc for 45 minutes-1 hour.

First make a red wine syrup:

Place the wine and sugar in a saucepan and reduce by two thirds until a thick syrup, save a little back for decorating the dish.

To assemble:

Place fig halves on the top of each cake portion, drizzle the red wine syrup on the plate, sprinkle crushed hazelnuts around then add a scoop of the red wine ripple ice cream.

Poached pears with mulled wine, lemon balm ice cream and mulled wine shot

Ingredients

FOR THE PEARS:

4 commis pears

Half bottle red wine

250g caster sugar

Zest and juice of 2 oranges

1 cinnamon stick

1 vanilla pod, split

3 cloves

6 juniper berries, crushed

2 star anise

For the lemon balm ice cream recipe see our ice cream recipe on page 160.

Method

For the pears:

Peel and core the pears. Place all the remaining ingredients in a saucepan and bring to the boil. Turn down to a simmer and allow to infuse for 30 minutes.

Add the pears and cover with a sheet of baking parchment. Simmer the pears for 20 minutes. Take off the heat and allow the pears to cool in the liquid.

Place the pears in the fridge with the cooking liquid and allow to infuse for 24 hours.

Rhubarb Trio

Rhubarb crumble, ginger cake milk shake with rhubarb crisps served with rhubarb and orange ice cream.

Ingredients

FOR THE CRUMBLE TOPPING:

50g butter, cubed

100g flour

75g caster sugar

Half a vanilla pod

FOR THE RHUBARB CRUMBLE FILLING:

200g rhubarb

150g caster sugar

1 tablespoon water

Juice of half a lemon

FOR THE GINGER CAKE MILK SHAKE:

150ml semi-skimmed milk

50g double cream

1 tablespoon liquid glucose

50g Jamaican ginger cake

1 teaspoon lecithin

30g caster sugar

FOR THE RHUBARB CRISPS:

2 sticks rhubarb

40g sugar

40ml water

Juice of half a lemon

See our ice cream recipe on page 160 for the rhubarb and orange ice cream

Method

For the crumble topping:

Remove the seeds from the vanilla pod and place in a bowl with the butter and flour. Rub together until the mixture resembles fine breadcrumbs. Add the sugar and mix in well.

For the rhubarb crumble filling:

Chop the rhubarb into 2cm cubes and place in a saucepan with the remaining ingredients. Cook over a medium heat until the rhubarb is cooked. Taste for sweetness – if the rhubarb is especially sour, add extra sugar.

Place the rhubarb in the bottom of an ovenproof ramekin and top with the crumble mix. Place in a pre-heated oven at 170oc for 15-20 minutes until the crumble is golden and piping hot.

For the ginger cake milk shake:

Place all the ingredients in a saucepan and crumble in the ginger cake. Bring to the boil then turn down the heat and allow to simmer for 20 minutes.

Remove from the heat and allow all the ingredients to infuse for 1 hour. Transfer to a bar blender and blend until smooth. Pass through a fine sieve and then chill.

For the rhubarb crisps:

Place the sugar, water and lemon juice in a saucepan and bring to the boil. Turn down the heat and simmer until thickened slightly. Using a speed peeler or mandolin, peel off long thin strips of the rhubarb.

Dip the strips in the sugar syrup and place on a baking tray lined with baking parchment. Bake in the oven at 70ºc. If your oven will not operate so low, switch it on pilot and allow to dry until crisp. This should take about 2 hours.

Trio of strawberry

Strawberry and cream terrine, strawberry shortbread, and a strawberry fab.

Ingredients

FOR THE TERRINE:
FOR THE STRAWBERRY PURÉE:

500g strawberries, quartered

100ml water

150g caster sugar

2 and a half gelatine leaves

FOR THE CREAM LAYER:

Half pint double cream

Handful of mint leaves

2 and a half gelatine leaves

FOR THE STRAWBERRY SHORTBREAD:

60g caster sugar

2 large egg yolks

60g butter

85g strong bread flour

1 level teaspoon baking powder

Seeds from half a vanilla pod

Strawberries for topping

BALSAMIC REDUCTION:

100ml balsamic vinegar

50ml caster sugar

STRAWBERRY FAB:

300g Strawberry purée (made in the same way as the purée for the terrine)

300g double cream

70g egg yolks

50g caster sugar

50g hundreds and thousands

Method

To make the strawberry and cream terrine:
For the strawberry layer:

Cook the strawberries to a pulp with the sugar and water. Blend in a blender then pass through a sieve to make a fine purée. The purée should be the consistency of double cream.

Soak two and a half gelatine leaves in cold water for 10 minutes to allow to soften. Take the gelatine out of the water and squeeze out any excess water.

Gently bring the purée to the boil in a saucepan and then add the soaked gelatine. Whisk and allow the gelatine to dissolve, then pass the mix through a fine strainer.

For the cream:

Soak two and a half gelatine leaves in cold water for 10 minutes to allow to soften. Take the gelatine out of the water and squeeze out and excess water. Meanwhile place the cream and mint in a saucepan and bring to the boil. Once boiled, take off the heat and allow to infuse for one hour. Pass the mixture through a strainer to remove the mint leaves and then bring 100ml of the liquid to the boil. Add the soaked gelatine leaves, whisk to dissolve and then place the mix thorough a strainer.

To assemble the terrine:

Line a terrine mould with a layer of cling film ensuring no air bubbles remain and that the cling film is perfectly smooth in the mould as any creases will show when the terrine is sliced.

Pour a layer of the strawberry purée 1cm deep into the terrine mould. Place in the fridge and allow to set fully.

Once the strawberry layer is set, pour on a 1cm layer of the cream mixture and allow to set in the fridge for an hour. When set, repeat with the strawberry and then cream until you have all 4 layers. Keep the terrine in the fridge until ready to serve and then slice with a hot knife at 1cm intervals.

For the strawberry shortbread:

In a food processor, blend the sugar and butter until light and creamy. Add the eggs and vanilla and whisk in. Sift the flour and baking powder and add to the mix. Beat to combine into a dough. Place the dough in cling film and roll up into a sausage shape.

Place the dough in the freezer for 3 hours (It's easier to slice neat circles from frozen).

Slice the shortbreads into half centimetre thick rounds and then place on a baking tray lined with baking parchment. Bake in a pre-heated oven at 150ºc for 10-15 minutes. Place carefully on a cooling rack and allow to cool.

To make the balsamic reduction:

Place the ingredients in a pan and then bring to the boil, reduce by about half until you have a thick glossy syrup.

For the strawberry fab:

Place the cream and strawberry in a saucepan and bring to the boil, then immediately remove from the heat. Whisk the yolks and sugar together until light and pale. Add a small amount of the cream and strawberry mixture to the sugar and egg yolks and whisk together. Repeat with the remaining mixture a little at a time. Place in a clean pan.

On a medium heat, simmer the mixture stirring constantly. Being careful to ensure none sticks to the bottom of the pan, cook until it thickens (the mixture is ready when it coats the back of a wooden spoon). Do not allow the mix to come to the boil otherwise the eggs will scramble and the texture will be unpalatable.

Once cooled, divide the mixture between small dariole moulds or shot glasses and transfer to the freezer until frozen.

To unmould, dip the frozen mould or shot glasses in warm water to loosen. Coat in the hundreds and thousands.

To assemble:

Place a slice of the terrine on a chilled plate. Put a fresh strawberry on the shortbread and then drizzle with the balsamic syrup before adding the strawberry fab.

Chef's Secret
All three components to the dish make a great dessert on their own if you don't fancy tackling the trio.

White chocolate pavé and cherries, sherry and maple syrup reduction

Ingredients

FOR THE CHOCOLATE PAVÉ:

250g good quality
white chocolate

100g butter

125g double cream

FOR THE CHERRIES:

150g cherries, stoned

30g sugar

1 teaspoon water

Half a vanilla pod

FOR THE SHERRY AND MAPLE REDUCTION:

100ml good quality sherry

75ml maple syrup

Method

For the chocolate pavé:

Place a metal bowl over a pan of simmering water and slowly melt the chocolate and cream together, ensuring they are fully combined.

Cut the butter into small cubes. Take the cream and chocolate mixture off the heat and whisk in the butter until fully incorporated.

Pour into a shallow container lined with clingfilm and allow to fully set in the fridge. With a hot knife, cut into large slabs.

For the cherries:

Place all the ingredients in a saucepan and then cook over a moderate heat until the liquid is dissolved. The cherries should still be whole but soft.

For the sherry and maple reduction:

Place the maple syrup and sherry in a saucepan and reduce down by half until a thick syrup.

To assemble:

Spoon some of the maple and sherry syrup onto a plate. Place the pavé on the plate and arrange the cherries. Garnish with a few sprigs of lemon balm or mint.

Beef Stock

1kg beef bones

2 carrots, roughly chopped

2 onions, quartered

2 sticks celery, roughly chopped

1 tablespoon vegetable oil

8 peppercorns

2 dried bay leaves

3-4 fresh parsley stalks

1 sprig fresh thyme

Heat the oven to 200oc.

Put the bones in a roasting tin and bake until well browned.

Put the carrot, onion and celery in another roasting tin and toss in the oil. Bake until well browned.

Put the vegetables and the bones in a large pan and add the peppercorns, bay leaves, parsley and thyme. Cover with water.

Bring to the boil and skim off any scum that has formed. Cover and simmer very gently for 3-4 hours. From time to time, skim off any scum that forms. Strain into a large bowl and allow to cool. Chill overnight. Skim off any fat that has formed on the surface.

Piccalilli

This is about as far away from the stuff you buy in a jar as Sheffield is from John O'Groats.

Next time you're up in Scotland, take some to have with your oatcakes and cheese

400g pearl onions

250g carrots

500g cauliflower

250g diced apple

150g sweetcorn

250g cucumber

650ml vinegar

Half tablespoon turmeric

Half tablespoon

coriander seeds

15g crushed garlic

125g sugar

3 cardamom pods

2.5 tablespoon cornflour

1 teaspoon salt

150g wholegrain mustard

150g olive oil

Boil the olive oil, mustard, salt, cardamom, sugar, garlic, coriander, turmeric and vinegar in a saucepan.

Chop the vegetables into 1cm dice and break the cauliflowers into small florets of similar size.

Take 2 tablespoons of the liquid and mix with the cornflour into a smooth paste.

Add a small amount of the hot liquid to the cornflour mixture and whisk until combined.

Return to the heat and allow to thicken.

Add the remaining ingredients and bring to the boil.

Once boiled, take off the heat and allow to cool.

This will keep for 3 months if correctly stored in a sterilised Kilner or jam jar.

Bread recipe

1kg strong bread flour

30g yeast

30g sugar

50g soft butter

30g salt

1 pint water

Combine the sugar, yeast, and water and leave for 15 minutes.

Fold together the flour and salt. You can mix by hand or in an electric mixer. If kneading by hand, tip the flour onto a work surface and make a well in the centre.

Add the liquid and butter to the well and mix until the dough is formed and elastic.

Cover with a damp clean cloth and then leave to prove in a warm place for 45 minutes–1 hour 30 minutes until the dough has doubled in size.

Knead for another 5 minutes.

Cut into 2 large and 1 small loaves or into 3 for medium sized loaves.

Shape into loaves and then prove again until doubled in size.

Bake at 185ºc for 25–35 minutes.

Mayonnaise

Serves 4-6 (Ready in 15 minutes)

2 medium egg yolks

1 teaspoon Dijon mustard

300ml light olive oil

Squeeze fresh lemon juice

Pinch salt and pepper

Place the egg yolks into the bowl with the Dijon mustard and a little seasoning.

Whisk until smooth.

Gradually add the olive oil in a slow, steady stream, whisking constantly. You should have a smooth, thick mayonnaise that stands in peaks.

Add lemon juice to taste.

If it's too thick, whisk in a few drops of warm water to give a good consistency.

Tip:

You can also make this in a food processor, adding the oil through the feeder tube. It will keep in the fridge for 3-4 days.

Ketchup

18 ripe tomatoes

6 shallots, finely sliced

250g brown sugar

290ml white wine vinegar

1 tablespoon English mustard

1 teaspoon dried chilli

1 teaspoon celery salt

1 teaspoon white pepper

Cook the shallots and tomatoes in a heavy-based pan until their juices begin to run out.

Transfer to a blender and combine for a few seconds.

Pour into a fresh saucepan and add the remaining ingredients.

Cook gently, stirring occasionally until the ketchup is the desired consistency.

Taste and season with salt if required.

Ice cream

Our basic ice cream recipe will make more than enough for each dish, but as it's labour intensive it's better to make a large batch, you can then add your chosen flavour, here are our suggestions but why not experiment with your own.

FOR THE SABAYON:

10 egg yolks

300g caster sugar

200ml water

ITALIAN MERINGUE:

240g caster sugar

4 tablespoons water

4 egg whites

TO FINISH:

500g whipping cream, whisked to soft peaks

First make the sabayon:
Boil the sugar and water to 120ºc.
With an electric whisk, start whisking the yolks in a bowl then slowly add the hot sugar and water syrup to the egg yolks.
Keep whisking until the mixture doubles in size and is light and fluffy.

Then make the Italian meringue:
Boil the sugar and water to 120ºc.
With an electric whisk, start whisking the whites to soft peaks in a bowl then slowly add the hot sugar and water syrup to the meringue.
Keep whisking until the mixture doubles in size and is light and fluffy.

Bring it all together:
Fold 500g of the whisked whipping cream into the sabayon until smooth. Fold in the meringue and pour into a large tub and freeze.

To add your chosen flavour:
For red wine syrup, ripple through 40oml of the red wine syrup.
For rum and raisin add 125ml dark rum and 200g raisins.
For crème frâiche ice cream, omit 250ml of the whipping cream and replace with crème frâiche.
For the lemon balm add a good handful of chopped lemon balm leaves.
For rhubarb and orange ice cream cooking 300g of rhubarb with 100g of caster sugar and the juice and zest of 3 oranges. Cook until stewed then allow to cool. When cool fold through the ice cream.